ADULT READING SERIES

Challenger 6

COREA MURPHY

NEW READERS PRESS
Publishing Division of Laubach Literacy International
Syracuse, New York

About the Author

Corea Murphy has worked in the field of education since the early 1960s. In addition to classroom and tutorial teaching, Ms. Murphy has developed language arts curriculum guides for public high schools, conducted curriculum and effectiveness workshops, and established an educational program for residents in a drug rehabilitation facility.

Ms. Murphy became interested in creating a reading series for older students when she began working with adults and adolescents in the early 1970s. The **Challenger Adult Reading Series** is the result of her work with these students.

In a very real sense, the students contributed greatly to the development of this reading series. Their enthusiasm for learning to read and their willingness to work hard provided inspiration, and their many helpful suggestions influenced the content of both the student books and the teacher's manuals.

It is to these students that the **Challenger Adult Reading Series** is dedicated with the hope that others who wish to become good readers will find this reading program both helpful and stimulating.

A special note of gratitude is also extended to Kay Koschnick, Christina Jagger, and Mary Hutchison of New Readers Press for their work and support in guiding this series to completion.

ISBN 0-88336-786-6

EACH ONE TEACH ONE

© 1988
New Readers Press
Publishing Division of Laubach Literacy International
Box 131, Syracuse, New York 13210

Printed in the United States of America

Designed by Chris Steenwerth
Cover by Chris Steenwerth

Cover photo by Greg Vaughn

Table of Contents

Unit 1
The Movies

"Let's go to the movies." This is a suggestion most of us have either made or heard many times when we're trying to think of something to do in the evening. In this unit, you will be reading five selections about the movie world.

In the first selection, "It Don't Hurt Much, Ma'am," the author explores the differences between the way in which movies generally present heroes and bad guys being shot and the harsher reality of real-life shootings.

The selection in the second lesson, "Will Rogers," presents a picture of the life of a very popular performer in the earlier days of the movies.

The reading for Lesson 3, "Some Facts about Motion Pictures," gives a short history of the movies and explains how movies are made.

Why do people enjoy going to the movies? The author of the fourth reading, a short story called "We're the Only Colored People Here," offers one answer to this question.

From the number of movie magazines found in the racks at newspaper stands and in drugstores, it is easy to see that many people enjoy reading about the lives of movie stars. The reading in Lesson 5 is a selection from Jackie Cooper's book, *Please Don't Shoot My Dog*, in which he describes something that happened to him as a child actor.

Lesson 1

It Don't Hurt Much, Ma'am

It Don't Hurt Much, Ma'am

"Oh, Sam, what happened?"

"Nothing serious, Miss Ruth—Luke just picked up a little bit of lead."

"Oh, no!"

"Now, Miss Ruth, don't you fret. It's just a little ol' hole in his shoulder. He'll be up and about in no time a-tall."

Sure enough, in two or three days good old Luke is up and raring to get back to defending sweet Miss Ruth, the Bar-X ranch, and the honor of the old Wild West. And Luke's adventure and speedy recovery, with slight changes, occur over and over on the pages of western stories and on movie and television screens.

But what really happened to those gunshot heroes and bad guys in that wild period of loose laws and fast gunplay? The reality was quite different.

The terrible effect of a large-caliber bullet on the human body can hardly be understood by people whose knowledge of shooting is limited to movie and television westerns. The most common guns of the West were the .44 and .45 caliber revolvers. Bullet caliber is measured by the diameter in inches: the lead slugs for these guns were nearly half an inch in diameter. Such a bullet packs a powerful wallop, knocking the victim off his feet if it hits any solid part of the body. The victim doesn't just drop dead either, as the movies would have you believe. He often staggers backward some twelve feet before falling to the ground.

Another thing about western stories and movies is the matter of wound areas. Good guys are almost always lucky and get hit in the arm, the shoulder, or the upper part of the leg. Bad guys are much more likely to take it in the chest, abdomen, or back, which means that they are killed. And nobody ever gets hit in the face.

The reasons for this are not difficult to figure out. Most movie watchers are used to seeing bullet wounds that look like neat little holes. In reality, gunfighters were hit in the face fairly often, and the big lead bullets caused terrible damage to mouths, teeth, noses, and eyes. You can't show that on the family TV, no matter how bad the bad guy is.

The reason that heroes are so often hit in the shoulder is that this is fondly imagined to be a "safe" place. The fact is that except for fat men and weightlifters, you can't put a hole through the shoulder without a fairly good chance of striking a complex system of bones, tendons, blood vessels, and nerves. A shoulder wound from a high-caliber revolver could be not only extremely harmful; it could be deadly.

In the Old West, a large number of the wounds resulting from gunfights were in the abdomen. The arm, leg, and shoulder wounds so often enjoyed by heroes in the movies were normally, in real life, the result of poor shooting and did not occur any more often than the shooter could help. The gunfighter went for the biggest target, which was the chest or abdomen of his enemy.

If a gunfighter did manage to survive a gunfight but was wounded in the process, he still had to survive the medical conditions of the Old West. Doctors were scarce, and some of the doctors were not really doctors at all. All too often, a doctor in the Old West was anyone who chose to call himself a doctor. In reality, about three-fourths of the "doctors" in the Old West were quacks.

The showdown that ends so many movie and TV westerns, where two cowboys stalk down the street toward each other, good guy waiting for bad guy to go for his gun, was certainly a rare occurrence. Far more often, a man was shot without ever having had a chance to touch his gun. Jesse James was shot in the back; Billy the Kid died in a dark room without shooting back; Wild Bill Hickok was shot from behind while playing poker.

Only the other night, I watched an old Western on TV, and I kept wondering when the hero would get his harmless flesh wound. Sure enough, he gets shot in (what else?) the shoulder, and for a while it looks as if he is done for. Then, just before the enemy moves in to finish him off, the United States Army thunders to the rescue. Minutes later, there is our hero, sitting straight and tall in the saddle and riding away at the head of his own troop as if nothing has happened. Oh yes, he does have his arm in a sling.

Adapted from "It Don't Hurt Much, Ma'am" by James S. Packer. © 1971 American Heritage Publishing Co., Inc. Reprinted by permission from *American Heritage*, February 1971.

1   **About the Reading.** The author of "It Don't Hurt Much, Ma'am" describes life in the Old West quite differently from what we usually see in movies. Each statement listed below presents the movies' version of a situation in the Old West. Beneath each statement, explain how the situation normally occurred according to the author. The first one is done to help you. Write your answers in good sentence form.

1. In the movies, a hero quickly recovers from his wounds.

    In real life, the wounds were much more serious, and good medical help was scarce.

2. In the movies, a large per cent of the bullet wounds are in the arms, legs, or shoulders.

    In real life, a large number of the wounds resulting from gunfights were in the abdomen.

3. In the movies, the shoulder is presented as a safe place for a bullet wound.

    In real life, it could be deadly.

4. In the movies, gunfighters don't get shot in the face.

    In real life, gunfighters are hit in the face fairly often.

5. In the movies, the victim normally drops dead just after he has been shot.

In real life, he often staggers backward some twelve feet before falling to the ground.

6. In the movies, the enemies often confront each other in a showdown.

In real life, far more often, a man was shot without even having had a chance to touch his gun.

What do you think? Do you think movies should show situations as they happen in real life? Be sure to include reasons that explain your answer.

No, I don't. I think movies should be made how the producers want, and it shouldn't always be the real story.

2 **Which Word Does Not Fit?** Choose the word in each row which does *not* have the same meaning as the other words and write it on the line. Study the example before you begin.

1.	abdomen	belly	liver	stomach	_liver_
2.	crisp	humid	muggy	sticky	_crisp_
3.	ban	forbid	outlaw	suffer	_suffer_
4.	boost	haul	hoist	raise	_haul_
5.	border	diameter	edge	rim	_diameter_
6.	affect	comply	follow	obey	_affect_
7.	distressed	excited	fretting	worried	_excited_
8.	imagine	occur	pretend	think	_occur_
9.	edgy	exhausted	nervous	tense	_exhausted_
10.	convinced	eager	raring	keen	_convinced_
11.	complain	gripe	nag	plead	_plead_
12.	grave	important	petty	serious	_petty_

3 **Words That End with -*ment*.** To complete these sentences correctly, choose the best word from the list at the left and add -*ment* to it. Study the example before you begin.

advance
ail 悩ます
commit
confine 制限
discourage
encourage
engage
enjoy
enlarge
manage
measure
✓ ship

1. When the clerk informed him that the ___Shipment___ of fresh lettuce wasn't expected until next Tuesday, Uncle Adolf was annoyed.

2. Al ordered an ___enlargement___ of his girlfriend's photograph for his desk at work.

3. When thirty-year-old Gail shyly produced the ___engagement___ ring Jesse had given her, her mother burst out, "But you're too young to be thinking about marriage!"

4. Bobby was unable to complete the ___measurment___ exercise his math teacher had given for homework because he had lost his ruler.

5. Holly declared she would make a ___commitment___ to stop smoking if her husband, in turn, would agree to lose forty-five pounds.

6. After describing the symptoms of his ___ailment___, Walter was surprised when Dr. Getwell remarked calmly, "My dear fellow, your problem is not physical; it's emotional."

7. The sign in the hotel lobby read, "The ___management___ hopes you will enjoy your stay in Los Angeles."

8. Ms. Bond suddenly found little ___enjoyment___ in cooking now that everyone in her family was on a strict diet.

9. Because of the many opportunities for ___advancement___, Martha chose a career in sales.

10. Most of us need a little ___encouragement___ to put more effort into reaching our goals.

11. In spite of receiving many words of ___discouragement___ from his relatives, Charles decided to risk going into business for himself.

12. During his ___confinement___ in prison, John learned that, although he was surrounded by people, he was very much alone.

4 **Who Was Wild Bill Hickok?** Use the words listed below to complete these sentences which describe the life and death of Wild Bill Hickok. The first blank has been filled in to get you started.

afternoon	continued	insisted	✓served
badly	defending	murderer	several
breakfast	duty	officer	strolled
certainly	included	refused	thieves

James B. Hickok (1837–1876)

Known as "Wild Bill," James B. Hickok _served_ as a spy and scout for the North during the War Between the States. After the war, Hickok had several jobs in the West, including peace _officer_. Hickok was known for his great courage and skill with a gun. Although he killed many _thieves_ and outlaws, it is said that he never killed a man unless he was _defending_ himself or it was in the line of _duty_. Hickok was a very handsome man who was quiet in manner. He was _certainly_ not a bully, and his friends _included_ some of the outstanding men of his day.

On the _afternoon_ of Wednesday, August 2, 1876, Wild Bill was playing poker. _Several_ times during the game, Hickok asked one of the other players to let him have his wall seat, but the player _refused_ to move. Wild Bill, who faced the front door and was aware of the one in the rear, _continued_ to play uneasily. At about 3:00 P.M., a small man entered the front door, _strolled_ up to the bar, and then eased himself behind Hickok. There was a shot and the shout, "Damn you, take that!"

Hickok's _murderer_ was a man with whom he had played cards the night before. The man had lost _badly_. Hickok had _insisted_ on lending this man the money for his _breakfast_.

Second and third paragraphs from *The West of Wild Bill Hickok,* by Joseph G. Rosa.
Copyright © 1982 by the University of Oklahoma Press.

5 **Spelling.** To form the plural of these words which end in *f* or *fe*, you must first change the *f* to *v*. Then, if the word already ends in *e*, add only *s*; otherwise add *-es*. Study the examples before you begin.

1. thief   thieves
2. calf   calves
3. elf   elves
4. half   halves

5. leaf   leaves
6. loaf   loaves
7. shelf   shelves
8. self   selves

9. wife   wives
10. knife   knives

Lesson 2

Will Rogers

Words for Study

Will Rogers	Capitol	ancestors	regular
audiences	Oklahoma	Cherokee	government
popular	nowadays	arithmetic	travel
Alaska	funeral	Andrew Jackson	sightseeing
statue	stomachache	North Carolina	almanac

Will Rogers

One cowboy of the Old West who did become a movie star was Will Rogers, who was born in 1879. Rogers' cowboy background was not as a gunfighter. His skill was with the rope, and often he would do fancy rope tricks while he spoke to audiences throughout the country.

Besides public speaking, Will Rogers was in fifty silent movies and twenty-one talking films, wrote six books, and was highly popular on the radio. In 1935, Rogers died in a plane crash on the northern coast of Alaska.

A statue of Rogers stands in the United States Capitol in Washington, D.C. Another statue stands in his home state, Oklahoma. This statue bears the statement for which he was best known: "I never met a man I didn't like."

Here are some selections from *The Will Rogers Scrapbook* in which Will Rogers describes his birth in Oklahoma, his feelings about Indians, and his thoughts just before he set out for Alaska where he died.

* * *

I was born at our old ranch. It was a big, two-story house. I was the youngest and last of eight children. My folks looked me over and said, "This thing has gone far enough! If they are going to look like this, we will stop."

I was born because it was a habit in those days. People didn't know anything else. In those days, a doctor would bring you into the world for two dollars a visit and make good money at it. Everything you were born with was supposed to be buried with you. But nowadays, when you die all you have left at the funeral is scars and stitches. If you had a stomachache back then, the doctor cured it; if you have it nowadays, they remove your stomach.

My ancestors didn't come over on the Mayflower, but they met the boat. My father was one-eighth Cherokee Indian, and my mother was a quarter-blood Cherokee. I never got far enough in arithmetic to figure out just how much "Injun" that makes me, but there's nothing of which I am more proud than my Cherokee blood.

It was old Andy Jackson that run us Cherokees out of Georgia and North Carolina. Now to tell the truth, I am not so sweet on old Andy. You see, every time old Andy couldn't find anyone to jump on, he would come back and pounce on us Indians. But Old Andy made it to the White House. The Indians wanted him in the White House so he would let us alone for a while. Andy stayed two terms.

The Indians were for a third term for Andy, but he had to get back to his regular business, which was shooting at the Indians.

The government sent the Indians to Oklahoma. They had a treaty that said: "You shall have this land as long as the grass grows and water flows." It was not only a good rhyme, but it looked like a good treaty, and it was—until they struck oil. Then the government took it away from us again. They said, "The treaty only refers to 'water and grass'; it didn't say anything about oil." So the Indians lost another bet. The first one to Andrew Jackson and the second to the oil companies.

* * *

People ask me, they say, "Will, why do you run around? Why don't you stay home?"

I've got to travel. I've got to go places in order to see things to talk about. I don't want to fly all night on a plane just for pleasure—just to be there. It's to get around and see something and find out something, so when you do talk, you know what you're talking about. I like to do anything right now. So I am off on a little sightseeing trip. I got to go and see that Alaska.

You see, I have been working pretty hard on some movies. I been making a lot of faces lately. I have used up all my expressions two or three times. You know, us actors just got certain little expressions for hate, fear, and happiness. An actor is a fellow that just has a little more monkey in him than the fellow that can't act.

Anyway, it just happened that I almost had three movies right in a row. That means I will have a little time off to do a few things I been planning on. You see, after I finish a lot of work, I sort of begin to look up in the air and see what is flying over, and Mrs. Rogers, in her wise way, will say, "Well, I think you better get on one, you are getting sort of nervous." So I went out to the flying field at midnight in Los Angeles to catch the plane.

Adapted from *The Will Rogers Scrapbook*, selected and edited by Bryan B. Sterling, Grosset & Dunlap, © 1976 (pp. 11, 47), and Bonanza Books, [Crown], 1980 (pp. 11, 47).

1 About the Reading. Choose the answer that best completes the statement and write it on the line.

1. Will Rogers was born in _____(d)_____ .

   (a) Alaska   (b) Georgia   (c) North Carolina   (d) Oklahoma

2. Will Rogers was most proud of his _____(c)_____ .

   (a) acting   (b) rope tricks   (c) ancestors   (d) sense of humor

3. According to Will Rogers, his parents _____(b)_____ .

   (a) had planned to have a large family
   (b) thought he was a strange-looking baby
   (c) were hoping for a girl instead of a boy
   (d) wished their children had been born in a hospital

4. One group of people that Will Rogers pokes fun at is _____(c)_____ .

   (a) businessmen   (b) lawyers   (c) movie stars   (d) physicians

5. According to Will Rogers, the Indians wanted Andrew Jackson to be president because ____(a)____

   (a) he forgot about them while he was in office
   (b) he passed laws which improved their lives
   (c) he protected them from the danger of war
   (d) he was part Cherokee himself

6. A main reason for the government's breaking the treaty with the Cherokees who lived in Oklahoma was _____(b)_____

   (a) Andrew Jackson declared war on them
   (b) oil was discovered on their land
   (c) the Cherokees were unaware of their rights
   (d) the treaty was never more than just a pretty rhyme

7. Whenever Will Rogers worked too hard, he became _____(d)_____ .

(a) angry   (b) downhearted   (c) foolish   (d) restless

8. The main reason Will Rogers enjoyed traveling was that _____(X) (c)_____

_____ .

(a) he needed to get away from his wife
(b) his hobby was flying
(c) it gave him an opportunity to learn new things
(d) it was his only form of pleasure

9. During his life, Will Rogers was *not* a _____(a)_____ .

(a) gunfighter   (b) cowboy   (c) radio star   (d) writer

10. Andrew Jackson served as president of the United States for two terms.

He was president for _____(c)_____ years.

(a) four   (b) six   (c) eight   (d) twelve

2 **Arithmetic Problem.** How old was Will Rogers when he died? _____56_____

$$\begin{array}{r} 1935 \\ -1879 \\ \hline 56 \end{array}$$

3 **What Do You Think?** Do you think Will Rogers would be a popular movie star if he were living in our times? Be sure to give reasons for your answer.

No, because he was a hero in the old West, and he may not good at acting in a popular movie.

4 **Pleasure.** Will Rogers found pleasure in traveling. In what sort of things do the people listed below find pleasure? Study the example before you begin.

beaches
blood
broomsticks (ほうきの柄)
gossip
knowledge
libraries
✓mysteries
strikeouts
tips
touchdowns
wisecracks (気のきいた冗談)
worrying

gossip ~~worrying~~
worrying ~~gossip~~

mysteries	1. armchair detectives
tips	2. bellhops = bellboys
libraries	3. bookworms
worrying	4. busybodies
gossip	5. fussbudgets = fusser (ロげくかすひと)
wisecracks	6. jokers
knowledge	7. learners
strikeouts	8. pitchers
touchdowns	9. quarterbacks
beaches	10. sunbathers [eiする]
blood	11. vampires
broomsticks	12. witches

5 **Displeasure.** In what sort of things do the people listed below find little or no pleasure whatsoever? Study the example before you begin.

✓alarms
bears
budgets 予算
cave-ins
confinement (閉じこめること)
daybreak
grease and grime (油・よごれ)
haste (急も)
hisses and boos (いヒ言う.)
potholes (穴)
train wrecks
weeds

alarms	1. burglars
bears	2. campers
confinement ~~potholes~~ ~~train wrecks~~	3. convicts (囚人)
train wrecks	4. drivers
~~cave-ins~~	5. engineers
weeds	6. gardeners
grease and grime	7. housewives
potholes cave-ins	8. miners
hisses and boos	9. performers
haste	10. slowpokes (のろま)
budgets	11. spendthrifts (金遣いの荒い人)
daybreak	12. vampires

6 **More Work with the Ending -ment.** To complete these sentences correctly, choose the best word from the list at the left and add -ment to it.

conceal (隠す)
detach (分離する)
employ
govern
involve
misplace (置き忘れる)
mistreat
punish
require
retire
settle
wonder

1. Years ago, a common form of _punishment_ for children who said naughty words was to wash their mouths out with soap.

2. Lynne searched the want ads carefully for _employment_ opportunities because she wanted a job that offered higher wages.

3. Many physicians suggest that one _requirement_ for good health is drinking eight glasses of water each day.

4. Bob's _Involvement_ _detachment_ with the group of students who had started the fight in the gym led to his being expelled from school for three days.

5. Mr. Stuart was looking forward to _retirement_ after twenty-five years of working hard in a machine shop, so he would have time to devote to his hobbies.

6. An expression of complete _wonder ment_ appeared on Phil's face when the nurse informed him that his wife had just given birth to twin girls.

7. The manager's _mistreatment_ of the brand-new computer led to its breakdown, and a repairman had to be called.

8. The Johnsons blamed the _government_ for all their problems with money—even though they did not vote.

9. _Detachment_ _Involvement_ is a necessary trait for an umpire if he is to call the action in a baseball game fairly.

10. George's _misplacement_ of important papers got him into trouble at work.

11. When Butch's _concealment_ of stolen goods was discovered, he realized he would soon be arrested.

12. Jamestown, an early English _settlement_ in the New World, was founded in 1607 and named after King James I.

7 | **The Capitol and Capitals.** The Capitol is the building in Washington, D.C., where the Congress of the United States meets. The capitals listed below are cities which are the seats of government for the states in which they are located. Use a map of the United States, an almanac, or a dictionary to match these capitals with their states.

Boston	Denver	Lansing	Salt Lake City
Columbia	Honolulu	Nashville	Springfield
Columbus	Jackson	Oklahoma City	Trenton

1. The capital of Colorado is _____Denver_____.

2. The capital of Hawaii is _____Honolulu_____.

3. The capital of Illinois is _____Springfield_____.

4. The capital of Massachusetts is _____Boston_____.

5. The capital of Michigan is _____Lansing_____.

6. The capital of Mississippi is _____Jackson_____.

7. The capital of New Jersey is _____Trenton_____.

8. The capital of Ohio is _____Columbus_____.

9. The capital of Oklahoma is _____Oklahoma City_____.

10. The capital of South Carolina is _____Columbia_____.

11. The capital of Tennessee is _____Nashville_____.

12. The capital of Utah is _____Salt Lake City_____.

Lesson 3

Some Facts about Motion Pictures

Words for Study

separate	camera	standard	scenes
position	operates	widths	Europe
continuous	lens	millimeters	performance
persistence	operations	theaters	industry
image	celluloid	dialogue	capitalization

Some Facts about Motion Pictures

When we watch a motion picture, we are really seeing many thousands of separate still pictures. In each picture, the position of the subject is slightly different. Each picture is flashed on the screen for a fraction of a second, but we do not see the separate pictures. Instead, we see smooth and continuous movement because of a condition of the eye called *persistence of vision*. For example, when the eye sees an object under a bright light, the image of that object will persist for one-tenth of a second after the light has been turned off. In this way, each picture on the motion-picture screen is presented to the eye before the image just before it has faded out.

The camera used to take movies operates much like a still camera. In both cameras, light from objects enters through a lens and exposes the film. But a movie camera takes pictures at a much faster rate. The movie camera can perform a number of precise operations to produce the pictures, or frames, that appear on the exposed films. As the camera photographs a subject, it keeps stopping and starting the film and opening and closing the shutter. The shutter controls the length of time that the light strikes the film.

Film for motion pictures is a strip of celluloid coated with chemicals that are sensitive to light. Both black-and-white and color films can be used in a standard motion picture camera. Motion picture film is made in several standard widths, which are expressed in millimeters. Film widths for movies shown in theaters are either 35 millimeters (about 1⅜ inches) or 70 millimeters (about 2¾ inches).

Sound in a motion picture is recorded on a narrow band along one side of the film called the sound track. During the making of a movie, the dialogue, music, and sound effects are first recorded on separate tapes. These tapes are then carefully blended onto a master tape. The master tape is then recorded on the exposed film, making a complete sound and picture print.

The projector flashes the exposed frames of film onto the screen. The projector, like the camera, stops and starts the film twenty-four times each second. Each time the projector stops the film, a revolving shutter opens and a frame is flashed on the screen. While the film moves to the next frame, the shutter revolves and shuts out the light from the beam. The viewer's persistence of vision fills in the periods of darkness, making the action appear continuous. In reality, the screen is dark for a longer period of time than it is lit. If the images were projected continuously instead of as separate frames, the viewer would see the motion picture as a blur on the screen.

The screen used in movie theaters gives a clear picture with bright colors. The speakers are placed behind the screen so that the sound seems to come from the picture itself. There are twenty to forty holes per square inch of the screen to allow the sound to project through.

Motion pictures were projected on a public screen for the first time on December 28, 1895, in a Paris café. Two brothers showed their excited audience some simple scenes, including one of a train arriving at a station. Soon after this, movies were being shown in many of the cities in Europe.

In the United States, it was Thomas Edison who presented the first public showing of motion pictures. This occurred in New York City on April 23, 1896. The program included a few scenes from a prize fight, a performance by a dancer, and scenes of waves rolling onto the beach.

By 1900, motion pictures had become a popular feature in amusement parks, music halls, traveling fairs, and wax museums in many countries. At first, movies did well because they were something new. The sense of reality impressed audiences. When the screen showed ocean waves breaking on the shore, women raised their skirts to keep them dry. But audiences soon became bored with these simple scenes, and it seemed as if the motion picture was doomed to become a passing fad.

What saved the movies from becoming just another fad was that they stopped featuring simple scenes and started telling stories. One of the first films to tell a story was *The Great Train Robbery*, an eleven-minute American movie which described a train robbery and the chase and capture of the robbers. Made in 1903, this adventure film was a huge success. *The Great Train Robbery* was but one of the many early steps which have led to the billion-dollar industry that movies have become in the United States alone. And, as most people know, the center of the American film industry is Hollywood, California, which is often referred to as "the film capital of the world."

Adapted from *The World Book Encyclopedia.* © 1985 World Book, Inc.

1   **About the Reading.** Put the letter of the correct answer on the line to the left.

_(d)_   1.   Millimeter is a term used to express the __o__ of film.

        (a) depth   (b) height   (c) length   (d) width

_(b)_   2.   Celluloid is the _____ used for motion pictures.

        (a) color   (b) film   (c) sound track   (d) type of camera

_(d)_   3.   The length of time that light strikes the film is controlled by the _____ .

        (a) lens   (b) master tape   (c) photographer   (d) shutter

_(a)_   4.   "...the image of that object will persist for one-tenth of a second..." *Persist* means _____ .

        (a) continue   (b) improve   (c) lighten   (d) release

_(a)_   5.   Persistence of vision is a term used to describe _____ .

        (a) a condition of the eye

        (b) a need for glasses

        (c) motion pictures

        (d) the lens of the camera

_(a)_   6.   Because of persistence of vision, _____ .

        (a) the action in a movie appears continuous

        (b) the images need to be projected continuously

        (c) we are able to see many thousands of separate still pictures

        (d) we are able to sit through a movie even though we don't like it

_(b)_   7. "The movie camera can perform a number of precise operations..." *Precise* means _____ .

      (a) difficult   (b) exact   (c) interesting   (d) necessary

_(d)_   8. The sound for a movie is projected _____ .

      (a) from both sides of the screen
      (b) from the ceiling of the movie theater
      (c) from the projection booth
      (d) through the screen

_(c)_   9. Motion pictures were shown to the public for the first time in _____ .

      (a) Africa   (b) Asia   (c) Europe   (d) North America

_(a)_   10. The home of the United States film industry is in _____ .

      (a) California   (b) Massachusetts   (c) New York   (d) Washington, D.C.

_(d)_   11. At first, movies were popular because _____ .

      (a) audiences enjoyed the adventure stories they saw on the screen
      (b) audiences enjoyed the performances of the actors
      (c) they did not cost so much money as other forms of amusement
      (d) they offered people something new

_(c)_
_(a)_   12. What saved the movies from becoming a passing fad was that they started having _____ .

      (a) movie stars   (b) movie theaters   (c) plots   (d) sound tracks

                                 =Story

2   Synonyms. A *synonym* is a word that has almost the same meaning as another word. Match each word at the left with its synonym. Study the example before you begin.

ailment	*vessel*	1. container
ceaseless 不断の	*ceaseless*	2. continuous
commitment 公約	*raring*	3. eager
employment	*occurrence*	4. happening
enjoyment	*requirement*	5. need
nowadays	*uneasily*	6. nervously
occurrence	*enjoyment*	7. pleasure
popular	*commitment*	8. pledge 公約
raring	*ailment*	9. sickness
requirement	*nowadays*	10. the present
uneasily	*popular*	11. widely liked
✓ vessel	*employment*	12. work

3 **Antonyms.** An *antonym* is a word whose meaning is nearly opposite to the meaning of another word. Match each word at the left with its antonym. Study the example before you begin.

conceal (隠す)   disappear   1. appear

confinement (拘束)   conceal   2. expose (危険にさらす)

detachment   confinement   3. freedom

✓ disappear   persist   4. give up

irregular   detachment   5. involvement (包含する)

movement   short-lived   6. lasting

persist   unpopular   7. popular

separately   irregular   8. regular

serious   movement   9. rest

short-lived   separately   10. together

standard   standard   11. uncommon

unpopular   serious   12. unimportant

4 **Spelling.** Change the *y* to *i* and then add *-ness* to these words. Study the example before you begin.

1. sleepy   sleepiness   6. lovely   loveliness

2. ugly   ugliness   7. dusty   dustiness

3. dizzy   dizziness   8. greasy   greasiness

4. lively   liveliness   9. holy   holiness

5. nasty   nastiness   10. uneasy   uneasiness

5 **Words That End with -ness.** To complete these sentences correctly, choose the best word from the list at the left and add -ness to it. Study the example before you begin.

aware
calm
eager
√ fond
forgetful
forgive
graceful
great
loud
rude
serious
still

1. Since her childhood, Chris had had a ___fondness___ for Westerns, but her husband refused to go to any movie in which the characters were wounded or killed.

2. When the ___loudness___ of the sound track made Andrew's ears throb with pain, he asked the usher if anything could be done about it.

3. "Do not let the ___rudeness___ of a few customers keep you from treating everyone politely," the manager told the employee who had just been hired to sell popcorn during intermission.

4. The usher quickly begged the woman's ___forgiveness___ after he almost tripped her while leading her down the aisle to her seat.

5. The ___gracefulness___ of the dancers in the musical inspired Nancy to sign up for a dance class during her lunch hour.

6. A movie producer's success often depends on his ___awareness___ of the likes and dislikes of the movie-going public.

7. In his ___eagerness___ to get to the box office early, Carl foolishly left his wallet on the kitchen counter at his mother-in-law's apartment and was unable to buy a ticket.

8. As if in a trance, the audience sat in complete ___calmness___ *stillness* while the hero stalked his enemy in the deserted warehouse.

9. The actor was so impressed with his own ___stillness___ *greatness* that, even though no one had offered him a part in three years, he decided to throw a party to honor his past performances.

10. Aunt Joyce's ___forgetfulness___ was getting so bad that, even though she had been looking forward to seeing the spy film for two weeks, she drove to the wrong theater and sat through a boring monster movie.

11. Because the hero responded with total ___greatness___ *stillness calmness*, no matter how tense and dangerous any scene was supposed to be, Mr. Brady decided the movie was phony.

12. Despite the supposed ___seriousness___ of the scene in the movie, the audience could not help but laugh.

6 **Capitalization Rules: Part 1.** In order to capitalize words correctly, you need to know certain rules. Study the rules below. Then capitalize the words in the sentences which follow. The number at the end of each sentence tells you how many words need to be capitalized in that sentence. Study the example before you begin.

1. **Capitalize the first letter of the first word in a sentence.**
   Example: The more John read of the book, the more he enjoyed it.

2. **Capitalize people's names.**
   Example: Last night Mrs. Harvey visited Aunt Elizabeth.

3. **Capitalize the word *I*.**
   Example: After watching the late movie on television, I fell asleep.

4. **Capitalize calendar items.**
   Examples: days of the week . . . . Thursday, Saturday
   months of the year . . . . January, April
   holidays and holy days . . . . Valentine's Day, Easter

   Note: Do not capitalize seasons.
   Example: Of all the seasons of the year, I like spring the best.

5. **Capitalize place names.**
   Examples: parts of the world . . . . Europe, the Middle East, the North Pole
   countries and sections of a country . . . . Egypt, Canada, New England, the Great Plains
   states and provinces . . . . Oklahoma, Illinois, Ontario
   counties . . . . Stuart County
   cities and towns . . . . Seattle, Jamestown
   streets . . . . Main Street, Penny Lane
   islands . . . . Hawaiian Islands, Bear Island
   mountains . . . . Rocky Mountains, Mount Washington
   bodies of water . . . . Gulf of Mexico, Great Salt Lake, the Nile River, the Black Sea
   structures and public places . . . . the White House, Central Park, the Golden Gate Bridge, the Statue of Liberty

   Note: Do not capitalize *the* when it appears before a name.

1. John and Mary had their first serious argument when he wanted to go to Cape Cod for their honeymoon and she wanted to go to the Thousand Islands.   (6)

2. On the fourth of July, people crowded along the banks of the Ohio River to watch the fireworks display.   (5)

3. Roger had been to South America and Africa many times on business trips, but he had not yet visited any of the countries in Europe.   (5)

4. Mrs. Price always started her Christmas shopping in late October and had all her packages mailed by Thanksgiving.   (5)

5. On Good Friday, Dr. Lodge and her children attended the worship service at the church on Chestnut Street.   (7)

6. When Kate moved from her cramped apartment near Carver City Hospital to a huge estate on Riverside Lane, she felt as if she had entered heaven.   (7)

7. Ruth slipped the book about Andrew Jackson into her handbag so she would have something interesting to read during her flight to England on Monday.   (5)

8. Buddy couldn't wait until August when he would be camping in the Great Smoky Mountains for three weeks with Dr. Carpenter and his family.   (7)

9. Mr. Knight couldn't recall the number of his niece's home, so he just wrote Rosebud Lane, Columbia, South Carolina, on the envelope and hoped the letter would get there.   (7)

10. "I think I will spend the winter in Honolulu before I visit you in Vermont," said Uncle Steven, who had never enjoyed cold weather.   (7)

Lesson 4

We're the Only Colored People Here

Words for Study

owl	roach	yellowish	instance
usually	curiously	unpleasantly	crackly
protests	Negroes	Technicolor	support
resentfully	desperately	classical	hatred
smartly	special	cinema	consider

We're the Only Colored People Here

When they went out to the car, there were just the very finest bits of white powder coming down. It wasn't cold. Martha laughed happily to herself. It was pleasant out, and tonight she and Paul were very close to each other.

"Want it to be the Owl again?"

"Oh, no, no, Paul. Let's not go there tonight. I feel too good inside for that. Let's go downtown?"

She always had to suggest that idea with a question mark at the end. Paul usually had three protests. Too hard to park. Too much money. Too many white folks. And tonight she could almost certainly expect a no, she feared, because he had come out in his blue work shirt. But Paul nodded!

"We've never been to the World Playhouse," she said cautiously. "They have a good picture. I'd feel rich there."

"You really want to?"

"Please?"

"Sure."

The World Playhouse wasn't like other movie theaters. There was another theater in the same building where real plays were performed. People were strolling up and down the lobby shared by the two theaters, laughing softly, smoking with gentle grace.

"This must be intermission for the play," Martha whispered.

"I don't know why you feel you got to whisper," whispered Paul. "Nobody else is whispering in here." He looked around, resentfully, wanting to see a few, just a few colored faces. There were only their own.

Martha laughed a nervous, bold little laugh and spoke loudly, "There certainly isn't any reason to whisper. Silly, huh."

The strolling women were smartly dressed. Some of them wore flowers in their hair. They looked well cared for. They looked as though they had never seen a roach or a rat in their lives or gone without heat for a week. And the men were men, Martha thought, who wouldn't stoop to fret over less than a thousand dollars.

"We're the only colored people here," said Paul.

Martha hated him a little. "Oh, hell. Who in hell cares."

"Well, what I want to know is where do you pay for the tickets?"

"There's the box office. Go on up."

He went on up. It was closed.

"Well," sighed Martha, "I guess the picture has started already. But we can't have missed much. Go on up to that girl at the candy counter and ask her where we should pay our money."

He didn't want to do that. The girl was lovely and blonde and cold-eyed. She had her hands on her hips and looked very sure of herself. No one else was at the counter.

"Well, we'll wait a minute. And see..."

Martha hated him again. Coward. She ought to march over to the girl herself—show him up.

The people in the lobby tried to avoid looking curiously at the two shy Negroes wanting desperately not to seem shy. The white women looked at the Negro woman in her outfit and could find no special fault with it. But it made them think, somehow, of small rooms and small, close lives. They looked at her hair. They were slightly but pleasantly surprised. They supposed it was the hair that had gotten her that yellowish, good-looking Negro man without a tie.

An usher opened a door of the World Playhouse part and ran quickly down the few steps that led from it to the lobby. Paul opened his mouth.

"Say, fella. Where do we get tickets for the movie?" The usher glanced at Paul's feet before answering. Then he said coolly, but not un-pleasantly, "I'll take the money."

They were able to go in.

And the picture! Martha was so glad that they had not gone to the Owl! Here was Techni-color, and the love story was sweet. And there was classical music that entered your whole body and made your back cold. And the theater itself!

It was no palace, no such great shakes as the Cinema out south, for instance (where many colored people went every night). But you felt good sitting there, yes, good. It felt as if when you left it, you would be going home to a sweet-smelling apartment with flowers on little glittering tables, and wonderful silver on night-blue velvet in chests, and crackly sheets, and lace spreads on beds you saw in the department store windows. Instead of back to your kitchen apartment with the garbage of your floor's families in a big can just outside your door, and the gray sound of little gray feet scratching away from it as you drag up those flights of narrow, complaining stairs.

Paul pressed her hand and said, "We ought to do this more often. And go to plays, too."

Martha pressed back, smiling beautifully to herself in the darkness. Though she knew that once the spell was over, it would be a year, two years, more, before he would return to the World Playhouse. And he might never go to a real play. But she was learning to love moments. To love moments for themselves.

When the picture was over, and the lights revealed them for what they were, the Negroes stood up among the furs and good clothes and faint perfume and looked about them eagerly. They hoped they would meet no cruel eyes. They had enjoyed the picture so much, they were so happy, they wanted to laugh, to say warmly to the others, "Good, huh? Wasn't it swell?"

But this, of course, they could not do.

---

1 **About the Story.** Answer the following questions in good sentence form.

1. What kind of mood is Martha in at the beginning of the story?

   She was happy.

2. What kind of mood do you think Paul is in at the beginning of the story? Give an example from the story to support your answer.

   He was [in good mood] pleasant. Because he said, "Want it to be the Owl again?"

3. How does Paul act once they get to the theater? Why do you think he acts this way?

   He acted that he wanted to see a few colored faces.

   Because they were only colored people and he was shy.

4. Martha feels hatred toward Paul for his actions. Explain why she feels this way.

   憎悪

   Because she felt that he was a coward.

5. What does Martha seem to enjoy most about being in the movie theater?

   The picture and the theater.

6. Once they are in their seats, how does Paul's reaction to being in the World Playhouse change? Why do you think it changes?

   He enjoyed the picture and the theater, because he had never experienced them. (answer) (Everyone was the same while watching the movie.)

7. Is the ending of the story happy or sad? Be sure to explain your answer.

   Sad. Others were so happy, they wanted to laugh, etc., but Paul and Martha couldn't.

8. Does it seem likely that Paul and Martha will go to the World Playhouse more often? Be sure to give at least one reason for your answer.

   No. Because Martha knew that once the spell was over, it would be a year, two years, more, before he would return there.

9. Do you think this story was written recently, or do you think it was written a number of years ago? Again, use information from the story to support your answer.

   I think it was written a number of years ago. Because there was a expression of "Negro". It's the old word.

   Colored という言葉の方がよい

2 **Synonyms.** Match each word listed at the left with its synonym.

cinema
continuously
eagerness
engagement
instance
loveliness
mercy [mɔ́ːsɪ] 慈悲
precise
protest
recently
separate
usually

separate   1. apart

engagement   2. appointment

loveliness   3. beauty

continuously   4. ceaselessly

usually   5. commonly

protest   6. complain

precise   7. exact

instance   8. example

cinema   9. film

mercy   10. forgiveness

eagerness   11. keenness

recently   12. lately

3 **Antonyms.** Match each word listed at the left with its antonym.

beauty
bold [bóuld] (⑫大胆な)
clumsiness (⑩ぎこちなさ)
commotion (⑩継続的な動き)
coolly
discouraged
dull
imagined
politeness
rarely
sinfulness (⑩罪のあること)
softness

dull   1. glittery (@きらきら輝く)

clumsiness   2. gracefulness

softness   3. hardness

sinfulness   4. holiness

discouraged   5. hopeful

imagined   6. real

politeness   7. rudeness

bold   8. shy

commotion   9. stillness

beauty   10. ugliness

rarely   11. usually

coolly   12. warmly

4 **More Work with the Ending -ness.** To complete these sentences correctly, choose the best word from the list at the left and add *-ness* to it.

bitter
dry
dull
fresh
gentle
plump (太った)
polite
smooth
stiff (硬直は)
truthful

1. The ___*freshness*___ of the fruits and vegetables at the farmer's market drew customers from all over town.

2. The ___*politeness*___ of the well-mannered children who were collecting money to fight world hunger so impressed Mr. Bergman that he gave them fifty dollars.

3. Mrs. Darling enjoyed being able to feel the ___*smoothness*___ of her husband's skin after he completely shaved off his beard.

4. Ever since Ben's automobile accident, the ___*stiffness*___ in his left shoulder told him when it was going to rain.

5. The ___*dullness*___ of the movie caused Dick to fall fast asleep in the theater.

6. After the doctor told him that the ___*dryness*___ of Arizona's climate would greatly improve his health, Jesse decided to consider moving there.

7. Staring uneasily at her ___*plumpness*___ in the mirror, Sue realized that she had to do something about her weight, which meant starting a strict diet—tomorrow.

8. "In all ___*truthfulness*___ , Your Honor, I am not guilty of the charges brought against me," declared Van Porter, who had decided to defend himself instead of hiring a lawyer.

9. Neil was filled with such ___*bitterness*___ after suddenly being laid off that he vowed to go into business for himself so he'd never be treated like that again.
(解雇する)

10. Ms. Harvey's voice always had a touch of ___*gentleness*___ in it when she scolded students for not doing their homework, but they knew that she meant business.

5 **Spelling.** Change the *y* to *i* and add *-ness*. If necessary, review the examples in Lesson 3.

1. thirsty _thirstiness_
2. risky _riskiness_
3. crazy _craziness_
4. dirty _dirtiness_
5. noisy _noisiness_
6. nosy _nosiness_

7. bloody _bloodiness_
8. clumsy _clumsiness_
9. scratchy _scratchiness_
10. itchy _itchiness_
11. faulty _faultiness_
12. sneaky _sneakiness_

6 **Capitalization Rules: Part 2.** Study the rules listed below. Then capitalize the words in the sentences which follow. Don't forget the rules you learned in Lesson 3. The number at the end of each sentence tells you how many letters need to be capitalized.

6. **Capitalize the names of races, nationalities and languages.**
   Examples: races . . . . Indian, Negro
            nationalities . . . . American, Canadian, French
            languages . . . . English, French, Dutch

(7.) **Capitalize special events.**
   Examples: World Series, Washington County Fair

8. **Capitalize historical events and periods in history.**
   Examples: historical events . . . . Boston Tea Party,
                                                      Battle of New Orleans
            periods in history . . . . Stone Age, World War II

9. **Capitalize the names of business firms and brand names of business products.**
   Examples: business firms . . . . Erie Shoe Company, National Bank of Los Angeles
            brand names . . . . Technicolor, Coke

(10.) **Capitalize the names of organizations.**
   Examples: government bodies . . . . the Congress, the State Department,
                                      the Georgia Supreme Court
            political organizations . . . . . the Democratic party
            institutions . . . . George Washington High School,
                                      Memphis State University
            associations . . . . Girl Scouts of America,
                                      the Cleveland Indians

1. when he was on the construction crew working on the new holiday inn, mr. holland always stopped at the greek diner on forest avenue for a cup of coffee and a muffin before going to work. (8)

2. adam bought two tickets to the super bowl game, hoping that the team he liked best—the dallas cowboys—would be playing in it. (5)

3. ms. woods couldn't find any books about the huron indians at the spring valley public library, so she chose one about the pueblo indians. (10)

4. When his ford stalled in front of bush county courthouse, louis realized he'd never make it to his appointment with the loan officer at standard savings and loan on time. (9)

5. the free ride insurance company paid dr. springfield $75,000 when the gas pedal on her brand-new rolls-royce stuck, and she drove through the window of roger's fish market on perch street. (14)

6. "i know this probably sounds like a phony excuse, mr. brooks," steven said nervously, "but my little brother dumped his bowl of jell-o all over the report we're supposed to turn in tuesday on the war of 1812, and that's the honest truth." (8)

7. When the jackson family went to Washington, d.c., they visited the capitol and met several members of congress. (7)

8. while tony lived with his aunt martha in springfield for six months, he went to falls road middle school. (9)

Lesson 5

Please Don't Shoot My Dog

Words for Study

Jackie Cooper	assistant	yelp	silence
ability	standby	tantrum	description
Norman	costume	security	cornea
concentrate	ducts	holster	fluid
holler	favorite	direction	heartily

Please Don't Shoot My Dog

Many people imagine that the life of a Hollywood movie star is always exciting. However, like so many other things we imagine, there is much more to life as a Hollywood star than just excitement.

In this lesson, you will read a selection from Jackie Cooper's book *Please Don't Shoot My Dog*. Jackie Cooper began acting in movies when he was about eight years old; and, in the following selection, he tells what it was like, as a child, to work on the set of a movie called *Skippy*.

* * *

When we started working, I did what I was told. My grandmother was with me on the set. If I did a scene we were filming right, I was a good boy. If I didn't, she'd slap me. She didn't pinch me anymore because now I was old enough to tell my mother when I got home. But, somehow, getting slapped wasn't so bad. I'd just forget that.

Skippy was the picture that made me known for my ability to cry. I had three crying scenes in the picture. They weren't easy. The first crying scene came at the end of a long, hard day. The director, who was also my Uncle Norman, told everybody on the set to be quiet and let me concentrate on my work. My grandmother said, "Be a good boy and cry." They waited. I tried. No tears.

My uncle had a temper. He screamed, and he hollered. He shouted that it had been a mistake for him to have hired me, and he told his assistant to start getting the standby kid ready to replace me.

I suppose all of this had been planned to make me unhappy, so I would burst into good tears. Instead, it made me angry, and angry kids don't cry. I hit things and slammed things and maybe even broke things, but not one tear was shed.

It was a deadlock. As I waited to see what my uncle would do next, I saw a new figure on the set, another kid dressed exactly as I was dressed, in the Skippy costume. The idea that they would give my part to any other boy was enough to make me very sad very quickly.

I came apart at the tear ducts. They rushed me into the scene, and I did it, and then they gave me an ice cream cone, and Uncle Norman said I was a fine actor, and my grandmother said I was a good boy.

From then on, for a while, everything was fine. Uncle Norman kept telling me how important it was to my mother that I work hard because my mother was still having to work and she—as we all knew—wasn't in the best of health.

I worked hard, as hard as I could. But I knew there were two more big scenes coming up when I would have to cry. By then I understood how they had tricked me the first time, and I was sure that they were going to try to trick me again. So I made up my mind that when the time came, I would cry by myself.

Of course, when the time came, I couldn't. Dry-eyed, I faced their anger.

A short time before *Skippy* began, a friend of my mother had given me a little dog. I have always loved dogs, and this one was a favorite. I kept him tied to my chair on the set, and he mostly slept all day.

Uncle Norman said he was going to take the dog away. He said that if I finished work in time (which meant if I cried for him) maybe I could get to the pound before they put my dog away.

I smelled a rat. This was the trick they were trying to use to get me to cry, but it wasn't going to work. I stood there and watched as my grandmother took the dog, untied him, and carried him out. I heard my little dog yelp. I knew she had pinched him to make him do that. Again, anger, not tears. Another tantrum. I was so mad that I threw anything I could get my hands on.

Uncle Norman said okay, that was the end. If I didn't stop, he said, he'd have the security guard on the set shoot my dog. I said he didn't have the guts. Norman nodded to the security guard. I saw him draw his gun out of the holster and watched him as he went in the same direction my grandmother had gone with my dog.

The set was deathly still. I couldn't see them. Then I heard a single shot. It echoed a moment. Then total silence.

I could imagine my dog, bloody from that one awful shot. I began sobbing so hard that Uncle Norman had to quiet me down by saying that perhaps my dog had survived the shot, that if I hurried and calmed down a little and did the scene the way he wanted, we would go see if my dog was still alive. So I did the scene the best I could.

Later, of course, I found my dog totally unharmed, and Uncle Norman, my grandmother, and the security guard grinned at each other, proud of the little trick they had pulled.

Adaptation of pp. 41–43 *Please Don't Shoot My Dog: The Autobiography of Jackie Cooper*, with Dick Kleiner. Copyright © 1981 by Jackie Cooper. By permission of William Morrow & Company.

About the Reading. Answer the following questions using complete sentences.

1. Describe the relationship between Jackie Cooper and his grandmother on the movie set of *Skippy*. Be sure to include details in your description.   *make him act nice*

   She tried to make him act nicely.
   Uncle Norman, ~~my~~ his grandmother, and the security guard grinned at each other, proud of the little trick they had pulled.

2. Describe how the director managed to get Jackie Cooper to cry the first time.

   He said that he was getting the standby kid ready to replace Jackie, and tried to ~~make~~ made Jackie unhappy.

3. Describe how the director managed to get Jackie Cooper to cry the second time.

   He pretended as if the guard shot Jackie's dog, and told Jack that let's go to see the dog as soon as Jack finished the crying scene.

What do you think? Jackie Cooper mentions that he had three crying scenes in *Skippy*. You have read his description of only two of these scenes. What might have happened to make Jackie cry in the third scene?   *O.k.*

   The director might say that Jackie's mother didn't feel good and Jackie should go to see her as soon as he finished the third crying scene.

2 Compound Words.
A compound word is made up of two or more smaller words. Fill in the blanks of the following sentences with the correct compound words.

1. A _____(a)_____ is an actor or actress who stands in for a regular member of the cast if necessary.

   (a) standby   (b) standout   (c) standpoint   (d) standstill

2. In "We're the Only Colored People Here," Paul felt _____(d)_____ whenever he went downtown because there were so many white people.

   (a) outfitted   (b) outgoing   (c) outlived   (d) outnumbered

3. The actress was so _____(d)_____ about her views on X-rated movies that the producer warned her to keep her thoughts to herself or she'd never work for him again.

   (a) outclassed   (b) outdated   (c) outsmarted   (d) outspoken

4. If you have a pain in your abdomen, you have a _____(c)_____ .

   (a) earache   (b) headache   (c) stomachache   (d) toothache

5. The _____(a)_____ for those born in the month of April is the diamond.

   (a) birthstone   (b) cornerstone   (c) headstone   (d) sandstone

6. Several guests flattered their host, who wore a purple _____(d)_____ sweater and black leather pants, for his fine taste in clothes.

   (a) bottleneck   (b) breakneck   (c) crookneck   (d) turtleneck

7. The postman, alarmed by the dark _____(b)_____, hoped he would finish his route before it started to pour.

   (a) thunderbolt   (b) thunderclouds   (c) thundershower   (d) thunderstorm

8. Mrs. Parsons studied the _____(c)_____ posted by the front door of the bus station to see what time her granddaughter was due to arrive from Seattle.

   (a) timecard   (b) timepiece   (c) timetable   (d) timework

9. Hoping to avoid the heavy traffic, Ted took a _____(b)_____ route to the airport but missed his 3:15 flight to Detroit.

   (a) gadabout   (b) roundabout   (c) runabout   (d) turnabout

10. Glen was able to draw a _____(b)_____ sketch of the mugger in no time at all with the witness's detailed description.

    (a) backhand   (b) freehand   (c) overhand   (d) secondhand

11. At their weekly meeting, the _____(a)_____ was happy to inform the shopkeeper that the business should be out of debt by the Christmas season.

    (a) bookkeeper   (b) housekeeper   (c) storekeeper   (d) timekeeper

12. "Our scheme went like _____(a)_____," smirked the thief as he and his partners in crime left the bank vault with their loot and dashed to the getaway car, which was surrounded by twenty policemen with their guns drawn.

    (a) clockwork   (b) needlework   (c) piecework   (d) homework

3   **Word Families.** Use the words in each set listed at the left to complete these sentences correctly.

imagine
imagination

1. As an only child, Elizabeth's _imagination_ had been her best friend, but now she could not _imagine_ happily spending time by herself.

concentrate
concentration

2. Dr. Strand's powers of _concentration_ were usually in good working order; but he awoke with such a bad case of <u>spring fever</u> that he knew he couldn't _concentrate_ , so he called in sick.

operated
operation
operator

3. Herman dialed the _operator_ to get his mother-in-law's telephone number so he could let her know that his wife had been _operated_ on that afternoon and that the _operation_ had been successful.

assist
assistant
assistance

4. The restaurant owner said to the _assistant_ manager, "We must give the waitresses some more _assistance_ . Have Roy hire two people to _assist_ in clearing the tables."

secure = safe
security
insecure

5. Uncle Roy's lucky rabbit's foot was his _security_ blanket. When his three-month-old puppy ate it, he felt so _insecure_ that he raced to the nearest drugstore, bought another one, and put it in a _secure_ spot—on top of the refrigerator.

adventure
adventurous
adventurously

6. The stunt man was feeling so _adventurous_ that he ignored the warning to use the safety belt and _adventurously_ drove his jeep toward the cliff. It was his last _adventure_ for the next several months.

desperate
desperately
desperation

7. _Desperate_ for someone to talk to, Linda called a neighbor she barely knew and said in an excited voice, which she prayed did not reveal her _desperation_ , "Oh, I'm so glad you're home. I've been _desperately_ trying to get in touch with you for weeks."

persisted
persistent
persistence

8. "If you'll let me continue," _persisted_ the manager, who was trying to explain the rules to the new employees. "Just be _persistent_ in carrying out your duties here and your _persistence_ will be rewarded sooner than you can imagine."

[rɪzɛ́nt]
resents
resentful
resentfully
resentment

9. "Your _resentment_ over our not being able to afford a new car can't match mine," said Fred's wife _resentfully_ . "Think how _resentful_ I am when my own sister _resents_ driving me to the laundromat once a week even though it's on her way to work?"

appear
appearance
disappeared
disappearance

10. Despite the _appearance_ of the situation, the detective decided the strange _disappearance_ of the necklace was not the result of a robbery. He was sure it had _disappeared_ while Mrs. Martin's two-year-old grandson was visiting and would soon _appear_ again.

4 **Tears.** Use the words listed below to correctly complete this description of tears.

anger   ducts   emotion   fluid   occur
cornea   dust   eyelids   layer   result

Tears

Two glands, one over each eye, lie behind the _eyelids_ . They pour out their fluid

through several small _ducts_ located in the underside of the lid. When a person feels

some _emotion_ such as sadness or _anger_ very strongly, the

muscles around these glands may tighten up and squeeze out the _fluid_ we call tears.

The same thing can _occur_ when a person laughs very heartily.

Tears help to bathe the cornea, which is the tough outer _layer_ of the eyeball.

This tear fluid helps to clear the cornea of such unwanted things as hairs and _dust_ .

Tears also keep the cornea from drying out. If the _cornea_ does dry out, the

result is blindness.

Adapted from *The World Book Encyclopedia.* © 1987 World Book, Inc.

5 **Capitalization Review.** Some of the words in the phrases below need to be capitalized. Rewrite each phrase correctly. Study the example before you begin. Not counting the example, you should capitalize 20 words.

1. the merry month of may — the merry month of May
2. a roll of cherry life savers — a roll of Cherry Life Savers
3. 620 riverside drive — 620 Riverside Drive
4. her french book — her French book
5. the u.s. justice department — the U. S. Justice Department
6. a bowl of cheerios — a bowl of Cheerios
7. the university of iowa — the University of Iowa
8. the roaring twenties — the Roaring Twenties
9. a dodge truck — a Dodge truck
10. halloween pranks — Halloween pranks
11. the canadian flag — the Canadian flag
12. the oklahoma state fair — the Oklahoma State Fair

Review: Lessons 1-5

1 **Word Review.** Use the words listed below to fill in the blanks correctly. Don't forget to capitalize when necessary.

Alaska	dialogue	tantrum かんしゃく [téndən]
Andrew Jackson	habit	tendon 腱(けん)
Capitol	Mississippi	Thomas A. Edison
Cherokee	Salt Lake City	wallop = heavy blow [wɑ́ləp]
cornea	statue	yelp 鳴き声

tendon 　　　 1. a band of tough, inelastic tissue which connects a muscle to its bony attachment

tantrum 　　　 2. a fit of bad temper

statue 　　　 3. a form which is carved or cast in stone, clay, wood, etc.

wallop 　　　 4. a hard blow

yelp 　　　 5. a sharp, short cry or bark

cornea 　　　 6. a thick structure which covers the lens of the eye

habit 　　　 7. a way of doing something which is so common to us that we don't even think about doing it

cherokee 　　　 8. an Indian tribe which formerly lived in North Carolina and northern Georgia and is now settled in Oklahoma

Capital 　　　 9. the building in Washington, D.C., where Congress meets

Salt Lake City 　 10. the capital of Utah

Thomas A. Edison 11. the great inventor who presented the first motion picture to the American public

Alaska 　　　 12. largest state in the U.S.; it became the 49th state in 1959.

dialogue 　　　 13. the lines spoken by the characters in a play or the words exchanged between people in real life

Mississippi 　 14. the longest river in the United States

Andrew Jackson 15. the seventh president of the United States

Review: Lessons 1-5 　**41**

2 **Synonyms and Antonyms.** State whether the following word pairs are synonyms or antonyms. Study the example before you begin.

synonyms   1. assist——aid

Antonyms   2. construction——destruction

synonyms   3. disappear——vanish

antonyms   4. dry-eyed——tearful

synonyms   5. event——occurrence

antonyms synonyms 6. fluid——liquid

antonyms   7. merry——depressed

synonyms   8. noisiness——loudness

antonyms   9. politeness——nastiness 不愉快

antonyms   10. resentful——forgiving [rizéntfəl] @ 怒って

antonyms   11. roundabout——direct

synonyms   12. secure——unharmed = safe

Antonyms Sy   13. separate——detach

antonyms   14. truthfulness——sneakiness [snírki~] 卑怯なこと

antonyms   15. unwanted——popular

3 Suffixes.

The *-ment* and *-ness* endings you have been studying are two examples of suffixes. A *suffix* is a group of letters added to the end of a word which changes its meaning. Choose the word which best completes each sentence and write it in the blank. As you fill in the blanks, note the six different suffixes you use.

1. "You're a driving _____(b)_____ !" exclaimed the saleswoman. "You must have the patience of a saint and nerves of steel to ride with beginning drivers."

    (a) inspector   (b) instructor   (c) operator   (d) protector

2. The _____(d)_____ was so shocked when his lab assistant told him that the research notes had been stolen that he refused to speak to anybody for a month.

    (a) collector   (b) conductor   (c) governor   (d) inventor

3. The _____(c)_____ of the ham caused the customer to complain, "You know, you really should serve water by the pitcher, not the glass."

    (a) greasiness   (b) spiciness   (c) saltiness   (d) tastelessness

4. "This freezer has outlived its _____(b)_____ ," remarked Susan upon discovering that the chocolate ice cream had melted all over everything.

    (a) costliness   (b) usefulness   (c) uselessness   (d) wastefulness

5. Ms. Prince whispered _____(a)_____ into the telephone receiver, "Please get over here as fast as you can. I think there's a prowler in the den."

    (a) urgently   (b) securely   (c) tenderly   (d) merrily

6. "You don't _____(a)_____ expect me to believe you're two hours late for our date because you had a flat tire?" George snapped at his guilty-looking girlfriend.

    (a) desperately   (b) persistently   (c) seriously   (d) usually

7. The basketball player made up in _____(d)_____ for what he lacked in physical build, and he finally won a starting spot on the team.

    (a) difference   (b) insistence   (c) occurrence   (d) persistence

8. When the governor made a special guest _____(a)_____ at the dinner to raise funds for cancer research, the guests applauded him for his concern.

    (a) appearance   (b) assistance   (c) disappearance   (d) performance

9. "I can give you _____(b)_____ about caring for your skin properly," explained the doctor. "But unless you're willing to follow them, I'm wasting my breath, and you're wasting my time."

    (a) inspections   (b) instructions   (c) operations   (d) protections

10. "Did completing this exercise require a lot of _____(a)_____ ?" inquired the English teacher.

    (a) concentration   (b) desperation   (c) combination   (d) operation

kindness   loudness   happiness

treatment   prospector   importance

4 **Where Might You Find These?** Match the words at the right with the objects or places in which you would most likely find them.

cameras
Capitol building
concert halls
Europe
graveyards (墓地)
holsters (ピストルの革袋)
horror movies
kennels
Michigan
mines
Mississippi
Oklahoma
state capitals
theaters
track meets

theaters   1. actors and actresses

mines   2. cave-ins

Oklahoma   3. Cherokee Indians

concert halls   4. classical music

Capitol building   5. Congress

state capitals   6. governors

graveyards   7. headstones (墓石)

Europe   8. Italy

Mississippi   9. Jackson

Michigan   10. Lansing (ミシガンの州都)

horror movies   11. monsters

cameras   12. shutters

holsters   13. six-shooters

track meets   14. timekeepers

kennels   15. yelping dogs

5 **Review of Capitalization Rules.** Give two examples which show your understanding of each of the following rules. Study the examples before you begin.

1. Capitalize parts of the world.

   _____South Pole_____ and _____the Far East_____

2. Capitalize bodies of water.

   _____the Red Sea_____ and _____the Clear Lake_____

3. Capitalize people's names.

   _____George Bush_____ and _____Lorna_____

4. Capitalize the days of the week.

   _____Tuesday_____ and _____Thursday_____

5. Capitalize the months of the year.

   _____May_____ and _____July_____

6. Capitalize holidays and holy days.

   _____Christmas_____ and _____Thanksgiving_____

7. Capitalize the names of organizations.

   _____the Supreme Court_____
   _____the Harris County Court_____ and _____the Congress_____

8. Capitalize the names of nationalities and languages.

   _____Italian_____ and _____French_____

9. Capitalize special events and periods in history.

   _____the World War I_____ and _____the Stone Age_____

10. Capitalize the names of business firms and brand names of business products.

    _____Dillard's_____ and _____Gap_____

6 Compound Words.

A. Use two words from the box to form a compound word for each of the twelve descriptions. Use each word in the box only once and cross it out when you have used it. The number of blanks for each word tells how many letters are in the compound word. Study the example before you begin.

B. When you have finished, the first letter of each compound word, reading down, should spell the name of a U.S. capital city and the state in which it is located.

ball	black	blot	board	bringing	checker	clothes
hiker	hitch	holder	ink	jack	left	man	man	odd
off	office	over	power	sand	spring	under	up

<u>C H E C K E R B O A R D</u>   1. a game board with sixty-four squares on which chess is played

<u>o f f i c e h o l d e r</u> (公務員) 2. a person who holds public office

<u>l e f t o v e r</u> (残り物) 3. an unused portion of something, usually food

<u>u n d e r c l o t h e s</u>   4. clothes worn next to the skin, beneath one's outer clothing

<u>m a n p o w e r</u>   5. the workers needed to complete a task

<u>b l a c k j a c k</u>   6. a card game also called *21*

<u>u p b r i n g i n g</u>   7. the rearing and training received during childhood

<u>s a n d m a n</u>   8. a character in fairy tales who puts children to sleep by sprinkling sand in their eyes

<u>o d d b a l l</u> (変わり者)   9. a person who behaves or thinks in a way that most other people consider strange

<u>h i t c h h i k e r</u>   10. one who travels by getting free rides along the road

<u>i n k b l o t</u> (インクの染み)   11. a blotted pattern of spilled ink

<u>o f f s p r i n g</u>   12. the children in a family

City: <u>C o l u m b u s</u>

State: <u>O h i o</u>

Unit 2
Work

Although movies and other forms of entertainment may be the high spots of our week, it is in the world of work that men and women spend much of their time each day. In this unit, the subject of work is explored.

It is a sad fact, but recent studies have shown that many Americans do not like their jobs. During the Great Depression of the 1930s, however, thousands of American workers were faced with a situation that was much worse than not liking their jobs. They lost their jobs and were not able to find other work. In the reading in Lesson 6, "Voices from the Great Depression," you will learn how some people responded to this very difficult time in American history.

The Lesson 7 reading, "When John Quincy Adams Lost His Job," describes how one man reacted when he lost his job. It wasn't just any old job that he lost, for John Quincy Adams was the sixth President of the United States.

The readings for both Lessons 8 and 9 are taken from a very helpful book called *What Color Is Your Parachute?* Believe it or not, these readings are also about jobs. In Lesson 8, "Looking for a Job," the author offers some helpful hints about finding work. In Lesson 9, "The Job Interview," the author gives advice about how to prepare for that meeting which many people dread—the job interview.

The selection in Lesson 10 is taken from *The Adventures of Tom Sawyer*. In this reading, Mark Twain shows us how Tom Sawyer handled the situation when he had a job to do but didn't feel like working.

Lesson 6

Voices from the Great Depression

Words for Study

crisis	enrolled	razor	preferred
we'd	college	ashamed	excellent
possessions	caseworker	General	references
deposit	psychiatrist	terrified	application
foreman	suicide	Italian	interview

Voices from the Great Depression

The Great Depression of the 1930s was a period of great crisis in American history. By 1932, the unemployed numbered upward of thirteen million. At least a million, perhaps as many as two million, wandered around the country in a fruitless search for work.

Here are the stories of just a few of the people who lived through these hard times.

Louis Banks, a man forced to be a hobo: 1929 was pretty bad. I hoboed, I bummed, I begged for a nickel to get somethin' to eat. When I was hoboing, I would lay on the side of the tracks and wait until I could see the train comin'. I would always carry a bottle of water and a piece of bread in my pocket, so I wouldn't starve on the way. I would ride all day and all night long in the hot sun. I'd ride atop a boxcar.

Everybody was poor. We used to take a big pot and cook food, cabbage, meat and beans together. We all set together, we made a tent. Twenty-five or thirty would be out on the side of the rail. They didn't have no mothers or sisters, they didn't have no home, they were dirty, they didn't have no food, they didn't have anything.

Peggy Terry, a woman whose family had moved from Kentucky to Oklahoma City to look for work: I first noticed the difference when we'd come home from school in the evening. My mother would send us to the soup line. We were never allowed to cuss. If you happened to be one of the first ones in line, you didn't get anything but the water that was on top. We'd ask the guy dishing out the soup to please dip down to get some meat and potatoes from the bottom of the kettle. But he wouldn't do it. So we learned to cuss. We'd say: "Dip down, goddammit."

My dad finally got a bonus and bought a used car for us to come back to Kentucky in. He said to us kids: "All of you get in the car. I want to take you and show you something." On the way, he talked about how life had been tough for us, and he said: "If you think it's been rough for us, I want you to see people that really had it rough." He took us to a place that was not to be believed.

Here were all these people living in old, rusted-out car bodies. I mean that was their home. There were people living in shacks made of orange crates. One family with a whole lot of kids were living in a piano box. This wasn't just a little section; this was maybe ten miles wide and ten miles long. People living in whatever they could junk together.

Hiram Sherman, an actor: It was rock-bottom living in New York then. It really was. You didn't count your possessions in terms of money in the bank. You counted on the fact that you had a row of empty milk bottles because these were

---

From *Hard Times: An Oral History of the Great Depression*, by Studs Terkel. Copyright © 1970 by Studs Terkel. Reprinted by permission of Pantheon Books, a Division of Random House, Inc.

cash. They could be turned in for a nickel deposit and that would get you on the subway. If you took any stock in yourself, you looked to see how many milk bottles you had. Two bottles: one could get you uptown, one could get you back.

Justin McCarthy, a worker in a Ford assembly plant: I sandpapered all the right-hand fenders at the Ford plant. I was paid five dollars a day. When I went to work in January, we were turning out 232 cars a day. When I was fired, four months later, we were turning out 535. Without any extra help and no increase in pay. If you wanted to go to the toilet, you had to get permission from the foreman. If he couldn't get somebody to take your place, you held it.

I made the mistake of telling the foreman I had enrolled in night courses at a local college. He said, "Mr. Ford isn't paying people to go to college. You're fired."

Mick Shufro, Assistant Director of the Chicago Housing Authority: I remember a mother of nine children was receiving two quarts of milk. Because of a budget crisis, she was cut down to one quart. She raised hell at the relief station. The caseworker wrote her up as crazy and sent her to a psychiatrist. The psychiatrist responded as few did at the time. He said "When this woman stops reacting the way she does, let me know. Then she would be truly insane."

Ben Isaacs, a door-to-door salesman: We tried to struggle along living day by day. Then I couldn't pay the rent. I had a little car, but I couldn't pay no license for it. I sold it for fifteen dollars in order to buy some food for the family. I didn't even have money to buy a pack of cigarettes, and I was a smoker. I didn't have a nickel in my pocket.

Finally people started to talk me into going into the relief. I didn't want to go on relief. Believe me, when I was forced to go to the office of the relief, the tears were running out of my eyes. I couldn't bear myself to take money from anybody for nothing. If it wasn't for my kids—I tell you the truth—many a time it came to my mind to go commit suicide. But somebody has to take care of those kids.

Wherever I went to get a job, I couldn't get no job. I went around selling razor blades and shoelaces. There was a day I would go over all the streets and come home with fifty cents, making a sale. That kept going until 1940. 1939 the war started. Things started to get a little better. My wife found a job in a restaurant for twenty dollars a week. Right away, I sent a letter to the relief people: I don't think I would need their help anymore. I was disgusted with relief, so ashamed. I couldn't face it anymore.

General Robert E. Wood, President of Sears, Roebuck: 1931 was worst of all. We cut, including myself. I started with a salary cut. We had to cut or we'd have gone out of business. We had to lay off thousands of people. It was terrible. I used to go through the halls of the building and these little girls—they were all terrified. I remember one Italian girl I called in. She had a family of ten—father, mother, and eight children. She was the only one working. It was terrible. But we had to lay 'em off. I could see how frightened to death they were.

1 **About the Reading.** Put the letter of the best answer in the blank on the left.

_(b)_ 1. The introduction states that many people "wandered around the country in a fruitless search for work." *Fruitless* means _____ .
(a) desperate
(b) showing no results
(c) seeking employment on farms
(d) praying for the right job offer

_(b)_ 2. Louis Banks probably became a hobo because he _____ .
(a) enjoyed traveling
(b) could not find a steady job
(c) preferred not to be tied down
(d) did not like to eat alone

_(c)_ 3. From the selection about Peggy Terry, the reader can conclude that Peggy _____ .
(a) was an only child
(b) enjoyed living in Oklahoma City
(c) lived in a house or apartment
(d) never went hungry

_(a)_ 4. According to Hiram Sherman, it cost _____ to ride the subway in New York during the Great Depression.
(a) a nickel   (b) a dime   (c) a quarter   (d) fifty cents

_(d)_ 5. From the selection about Justin McCarthy, the reader can conclude that Justin _____ .
(a) had not graduated from high school
(b) was friends with the foreman
(c) was married
(d) had to work harder the longer he worked at the Ford plant

_(d)_ 6. Mick Shufro thinks that the psychiatrist he tells about _____ .
(a) did not understand the woman's problem
(b) should have felt ashamed of himself
(c) was a better psychiatrist than most he knew
(d) should have been fired

_(a)_ 7. According to Ben Issacs, the hard times eased up somewhat when _____ .
(a) World War II started
(b) jobs were less scarce
(c) people sold their possessions
(d) food prices went down

_(d)_ 8. According to General Robert E. Wood, the main reaction of the people whom he had to lay off was _____ .
(a) resentment   (b) impatience   (c) nastiness   (d) fear

2 **What Do You Think?** If you had been alive during the Great Depression, what do you think your life would have been like? Be sure to include details in your description.

> We live in a rental house, and so we have to go out of it, because we can't pay anymore.
> We try to find an appartment, but can't live there, it's too expensive for us. Then we build up a tent house with little housewares.
> We are always hungry, and get thin.

3 **Synonyms.** On the blank to the right, write the synonym for the first word in the line. Study the example before you begin.

1. **possess:**	borrow	deserve	desire	own	own
2. **doubtful:**	uncertain	uncommon	unfair	unwilling	uncertain
3. **ashamed:**	sensitive	outclassed	disgraced	terrified	disgraced
4. **permit:**	allow	consider	deposit	enroll	allow
5. **recently:**	generally	hourly	lately	seldom	lately
6. **terrify:**	disturb	frighten	injure	reject	frighten
7. **easygoing:**	careless	normal	outgoing	relaxed	relaxed
8. **alter:**	assist	change	repair	undo	change
9. **gloomy:**	cold-eyed	dejected	hearty	serious	dejected
10. **scatter:**	disable	discharge	disperse	dispose	disperse
11. **moral:**	story	ending	fable	lesson	fable lesson
12. **concept:**	idea	law	rule	suggestion	idea

4   **The Suffix -ful.** To complete these sentences, chose the correct word from the list at the left and add -ful to it. Study the example before you begin.

event
fear
force
plate
play
regret
√scoop

1. Mrs. Solly asked the clerk to measure out a __Scoopful__ of blueberry jellybeans which she planned to share with her son.

2. Jackie's __playful__ new puppy nipped at her heels as they ran through the park.

3. Winning the contest certainly made Dennis's day very __eventful__ , but he was so __fearful__ of becoming seasick that he turned down the all-expenses-paid cruise to Hawaii.

4. "You have excellent references," explained Ms. Thor as she skimmed Philip's application, "but I'm afraid you just aren't __forceful__ enough to be a foreman; our workers would take advantage of you in a minute."

5. "Why should I feel __regretful__ ?" snapped the waitress to her manager. "If the customer had behaved politely, I would never have dumped the __plateful__ of French fries in his lap."

5 **The Suffix -less.** To complete these sentences, choose the correct word from the list at the left and add -less to it. Study the example before you begin.

age
blame (非難する)
fear
heart
meaning
mind
✓shame

1. The ___shameless___ traitor just shrugged his shoulders when, during an interview, a reporter called him a disgrace to his country.

2. "How can you be so ___mindless___ !" exclaimed Jane when her former *heartless = without feeling*

   boss refused to give her a good reference because he couldn't bear the thought of her working for anyone else.

3. Ninety-one-year-old Mr. Finn had so much energy that his neighbors regarded him as one of those ___ageless___ human beings who would outlive them all.

4. "This discussion is ___meaningless___," Anne said to her business partners, "if you refuse to see that we aren't entirely ___blameless___ for the terrible working conditions around here."

5. When Hiram dashed into the burning animal shelter to rescue the trapped kittens, some bystanders praised him as a ___fearless___ hero. Others, *mindless*

   however, called him ___heartless___ because the odds of his getting out of 強い愛好

   the building alive were very slim. *without thinking*

6 **Review of Capitalization Rules.** Capitalize the words in the following sentences correctly. The number at the end of each sentence tells you how many words to capitalize. If necessary, review the rules you've studied so far in Lessons 3 and 4.

More about the Great Depression

1. october 29, 1929, is known as black tuesday in american history books; that was the day the stock market on wall street in new york city hit bottom. (9)

2. during the first and worst years of the depression, the people turned to washington for help; and when the president of the united states did not offer the necessary assistance, they voted him out of office. (5)

3. in 1931, a man who worked for the public school system in chicago begged the governor of illinois to help feed the city's children during the summer. (3)

4. in the 1930s, our main meal was something uncle robert called *shipwreck*: heated campbell's tomato soup poured over ritz crackers. (5)

5. not only was there no money during the great depression; there was no rain. in georgia, a negro was paid ten dollars to pray for rain. in new york, an indian tribe revived their rain-prayer dance for the first time in forty years. (10)

6. a texas farmer, angry because his crops were drying up from lack of rain, jumped on his tractor and began to drive in circles around his fields. as he drove, he spluttered, "i know this won't do any good, but i've got to do something." (5)

7. on december 7, 1941, americans were shocked to learn that the japanese had bombed pearl harbor in hawaii. shortly afterward, congress declared war on japan. (10)

8. the great depression came to an end when congress voted huge sums of money for producing goods that the united states would need to fight in world war II. (8)

Lesson 7 ━━━━━━━━━━━━━━━━━━━━━━━━━━

When John Quincy Adams Lost His Job

Words for Study

Quincy	fierce	symbol	usual
election	furies	pimples	James Polk
desirable	ex-president	promise	coma
series	slavery	Alabama	tomb
undertook	experience	union	classified
trickled	abuse	victory	abbreviation

When John Quincy Adams Lost His Job

In 1828, John Quincy Adams lost his job. He had been president of the United States for four years, and now he had been defeated in the 1828 election by Andrew Jackson. Losing the election greatly depressed John Quincy Adams who could not adjust to this painful defeat. He shut himself off from the world in his Quincy, Massachusetts, home and wrote, "I have no real reason for wishing to live when every thought I have about the future makes death desirable." Bitterly, Adams complained, "My whole life has been a series of disappointments. I can scarcely remember a single instance of success in anything that I ever undertook."

Short, overweight, and almost completely bald, John Quincy Adams was old before his time. He had many ailments. His hand shook almost beyond control when he wrote. He complained about his bloodshot eyes which were so weak and swollen that tears often trickled from the corners. His voice, which was always shrill, tended to crack whenever he spoke. He slept little and badly, and his diary was filled with complaints of "disturbed sleep—full of tossings."

Another problem was Adams's temper, which was extremely short. One Congressman described it as "fierce as ten furies, terrible as hell." Adams himself admitted in his diary that he was forever having to work hard to control his temper.

Then, in 1830, a group of devoted friends convinced Adams to run for Congress. Adams felt as if he had been born a new man. He was sixty-three years old, a retired president, and the son of the second president of the United States. Never before and never since has a former president of the United States run for Congress.

Adams won his election and entered Congress. There he would serve for the next eighteen years—until the end of his life. Instead of the peace and quiet sought by George Washington and other ex-presidents, John Quincy Adams would carve out a brand-new career for himself. Though he had carefully avoided the slavery issue during his White House years, Adams now plunged into it with all his heart, drawing much anger and debate around his head. No other former president would experience such abuse. Newspapers even branded him the "Mad Man from Massachusetts."

John Quincy Adams became a one-man symbol of the struggle against slavery. Day after day, with surprising energy, he held the floor of Congress, his shrill voice slashing away at his enemies. Even though he suffered from a bad cough, pimples, and boils, he would arise early each morning to prepare his work for the day.

Adams's hard work to end slavery brought an increasing flood of angry and threatening letters to his desk. "Your damned guts will be cut out in the dark," warned a writer from Georgia. "On the first day of May, I promise to cut your throat from ear to ear," threatened an Alabama writer.

In spite of these dark threats, Adams worked on in his efforts to end slavery which he had once described as "the great and foul stain upon the North American Union." Slowly but surely, his efforts began to win the praise of others who were also devoted to ending slavery in the United States.

In 1842, the South suffered its first important defeat in Congress—a defeat that had been brought about mainly through the work of John Quincy Adams. In a letter to his wife, Adams's assistant described this Southern defeat: "This is the first victory over the slaveholders in a body ever yet gained since the founding of the government and from this time their downfall takes its date."

On Monday, February 21, 1848, Adams, now eighty-one, reached Congress early as usual. James Polk, who was now president of the United States, had just received the treaty of peace with Mexico. A roll call was going on, and the House was filled with clatter. Suddenly, a member seated near Adams saw the old man's face redden, while his right hand clutched at the corner of his desk. Then he slumped over.

Someone cried out and caught Adams in his arms. They carried him to the cleared area in front of the Speaker's table, where he was placed on a couch and moved to the Speaker's room. For a few minutes Adams revived. Leaning close, a fellow Congressman heard Adams say, "This is the end of earth, but I am at peace."

Meanwhile, Adams's wife arrived, but Adams had fallen into a coma and gave no sign of recognizing her. He remained in a coma through Washington's birthday and at 7:20 on the evening of February 23 passed away.

The service three days later was a great public event. Thousands of people filed by his coffin while he lay in state in the House. Southern leaders joined the North in paying honor to Adams. Then the body was taken to Boston, where thousands more paid their last respects.

Adams was buried in Quincy, Massachusetts—in the old family tomb in the churchyard. At the last moment a southern congressman in the funeral party stepped forward and, stooping before the Adams vault, called out, "Good-bye, Old Man!"

From *The Bold Brahmins* by Lawrence Lader. Adapted with permission of the author.

---

1   **About the Reading.** Put the letter of the best answer in the blank on the left.

_____ 1. The title of this reading selection refers to the job that John Quincy Adams lost. What job did he lose?

(a) mayor of Quincy
(b) congressman from Georgia
(c) governor of Massachusetts
(d) president of the United States

_____ 2. When Adams lost this job, he felt _____ .

(a) dejected   (b) fierce   (c) puzzled   (d) relieved

_____ 3. Then, receiving encouragement from his _____ , he decided to run for Congress.

(a) friends   (b) father   (c) wife   (d) children

_(c)_   4. While in Congress, Adams was called the "Mad Man from Massachusetts" because he _____ .

    (a) did not retire to peace and quiet as other ex-presidents had
    (b) did not take very good care of himself
    (c) fought to end slavery
    (d) had a terrible temper

_(b)_   5. Just before he died, Adams said he was "at peace." He probably felt this way because he had _____ .

    (a) succeeded in becoming famous
    (b) finished all he had set out to do
    (c) helped to end the war with Mexico
    (d) made important strides toward ending slavery

_(b)_   6. Adams was buried in _____ .

    (a) Washington, D.C.
    (b) Massachusetts
    (c) Vermont
    (d) New York

_(d)_   7. The southern Congressman who called out "Good-bye, Old Man" probably _____ .

    (a) did not know Adams's name
    (b) thought Adams was too old to serve in Congress
    (c) thought Adams was silly not to retire after being defeated by Jackson
    (d) admired Adams

_(b)_   8. The author of this reading selection seems to _____ John Quincy Adams.

    (a) disagree with
    (b) admire
    (c) have been a personal friend of
    (d) lack respect for

An arithmetic problem. In what year did Adams become president of the United States? _18 2+5_

2 **Symbols.** A *symbol* is a sign that stands for an object or an idea. All words are symbols. One well-known symbol is the national flag. To most people, the flag of their nation means "my country." Below are two sets of commonly-used symbols. Match the symbols at the left with what they stand for.

broken mirror
four-leaf clover
striped pole
scales
skull and crossbones
Uncle Sam
yellow
CO_2
♫
O

_____*striped pole*_____ 1. barber shop

_____*CO_2*_____ 2. carbon dioxide

_____*yellow*_____ 3. cowardliness

_____*four-leaf clover*_____ 4. good luck

_____*scales*_____ 5. justice

_____♫_____ 6. music

_____O_____ 7. oxygen

_____*skull and crossbones*_____ 8. poison

_____*broken mirror*_____ 9. seven years' bad luck

_____*Uncle Sam*_____ 10. United States

This second set deals with animals which are used as symbols.

bat
beaver
bee or ant
dove
eel
fox
lamb
mule
owl
ox or bull

_____*owl bat*_____ 1. blindness

_____*beaver bee or ant*_____ 2. busyness

_____*bat beaver*_____ 3. eagerness

_____*bee or ant lamb*_____ 4. gentleness

_____*dove*_____ 5. peace

_____*eel*_____ 6. slipperiness

_____*fox*_____ 7. slyness

_____*ox or bull*_____ 8. strength

_____*mule*_____ 9. stubbornness

_____*lamb owl*_____ 10. wisdom

3 **Word Families.** Use the words in each set listed at the left to complete these sentences.

elected
election

1. After the _____*election*_____, the governor felt so exhausted that he

almost wished the voters hadn't _____*elected*_____ him to serve a second term.

adjust
adjustments

2. "I've had to make a lot of _adjustments_ in my time," wept Grandfather to his grandson, "but I don't think I'll ever _adjust_ to living without your grandmother."

refer
reference

3. "In _reference_ to your question about John Quincy Adams," responded the teacher to her students, "let's _refer_ to our history book."

prefer
preference

4. When the waiter asked Peggy if she would _prefer_ French or Italian dressing on her tossed salad, she replied, "I don't really have a _preference_."

slippery
slipperiness

5. The weather forecaster, who was predicting freezing rain, told his listeners, "Those of you who walk to work, watch out for the _slippery_ sidewalks. And those of you who drive, be on the lookout for the _slipperiness_ of the roads."

hearty
heartily
heartless

6. "After such a _hearty_ meal at the Marshes' housewarming party," laughed Rocco _heartily_, "I think it would be _heartless_ of us not to invite them to our Saturday picnic."

stubborn
stubbornly
stubbornness

7. "I am not _stubborn_!" Isaac insisted _stubbornly_ after his daughter had stated that the family's crisis was caused by his _stubbornness_.

applied
applicant
application

8. While filling out the _application_ for the chef's position at Lowland Hotel, the _applicant_ asked the desk clerk if many people had _applied_.

coward
cowardly
cowardliness

9. "Not only has your _cowardliness_ in the line of duty cost many brave men their lives today," said the commander coldly, "but the _cowardly_ excuses you make to explain your actions make me realize that you're a _coward_ through and through."

usual
usually
unusual
unusually

10. "You just don't seem like your _usual_ self these days, Justin," commented his sister, who _usually_ didn't mind _unusually_ long periods of quiet but was becoming increasingly worried because Justin's silence seemed so _unusual_.

4   **Looking for a Job.** Most ex-presidents don't have to read the classified ads if they want to continue working. Most of us do. Study the following ads taken from the classified section of a daily newspaper and then answer the questions.

ANSWERING SERVICE OPERATOR - Good telephone manner a must, 7:30 a.m. - 1 p.m. Mon. thru Fri. Call 555-2226.	BUSBOYS PART TIME WEEKENDS No experience necessary. Must be 16 or older, for appt. call Rolling Hills Country Club 555-8381 (Closed Mondays)	DRIVERS, If you are seriously thinking of making driving your career. Apply in person: Carson's Yellow Cab, 155 Main St.	MANAGER needed for better ladies sportswear shop. Experience necessary. Phone 555-1977 for an appointment.
ASSISTANT SWIM COACH 5 days a week, hours 5-7 p.m., meets are held on Saturdays. Season Sept.-March. For details call YMCA 555-1000	CONSTRUCTION "Jack-of-all-Trades" Must have exper. in light carpentry & have ability to make adjustments & small repairs on call-backs. Phone 555-5100 days; 9-6.	GAS STATION Full Time Manager New Milford area Call Phil 555-0650	RESTAURANT-Sandwich-Salad bar person. 3 evenings per week, 3-10pm. Apply in person, Plain Jane's Restaurant.
ASSISTANT COOKS-4 shifts-week, will train. Ideal for students. Apply in person: Pickles Restaurant.	COOK wanted for Day Care Center, 10am-1pm., Mon-Fri. Call for interview. 555-2480	GRILL PERSONS—Full & part time. Good wages & vacations. Apply in person Combs Restaurant, 113 Mill Plain Rd.	SWIMMING POOL-Local pool company looking for young and strong person to help with pool construction. Call 555-0777 bet. 10am-5pm
BARTENDER, part time, days or nights. Apply in person: Cheers, 5 Elm St.	COUNTER HELP WANTED for auto parts store Apply in person between 1-4pm 139 Main St.	GROUND WORKER Needed for tree company. Will train if necessary. Good wages, call 555-8790.	WAITER—WAITRESS wanted for morning shift or supper hour shifts. Please apply in person, Windmill Diner, 14 Mill Plain Rd.

1. Because space is so tight, many abbreviations are used in classified ads. What do the following abbreviations stand for? Study the example before you begin.

   (a) Mon. _____Monday_____   (d) appt. _____appointment_____

   (b) Fri. _____Friday_____   (e) bet. _____between_____

   (c) Sept. _____September_____   (f) & _____and_____

2. Which ad states an age requirement? _____Busboys Part Time Weekends_____

3. Which two ads state that experience is necessary? _____Construction "Jack-of-all-Trades" and Manager needed for better ladies sportswear shp._____

4. Why do you think some of these ads state that the applicant must apply in person?

   _____Because employers want to know if applicants fit the jobs or not._____

   _____

5. If you had to work and these ads were the only employment opportunities open to you, which of these jobs would you apply for? Be sure to include reasons in your answer.

   _____I would apply for assistant cooks. Because I like cooking, and can be trained. And it's not a full time job, and I prefer that._____

   _____

5 Can You Crack the Code?

Each group of letters spells the name of an American president, but their names have been concealed by a code in which a new set of letters has been used in place of the normal letters. The code is the same for all the words. When you have guessed the name of the president, use these letters to help you figure out the names of the remaining presidents. The first item has been done for you to get you started.

JAMES POLK
1. B X C K G   W Z P S

GEORGE WASHINGTON
2. Y K Z O Y K   E X G U F T Y M Z T

JOHN F KENNEDY
3. B Z U T   Q.   S K T T K J L

JOHN QUINCY ADAMS
4. B Z U T   V H F T R L   X J X C G

ANDREW JACKSON
5. X T J O K E   B X R S G Z T

ABRAHAM LINCOLN
6. X D O X U X C   P F T R Z P T

JOHN ADAMS
7. B Z U T   X J X C G

THOMAS JEFFERSON
8. M U Z C X G   B K Q Q K O G Z T

JAMES MADISON
9. B X C K G   C X J F G Z T

JAMES MONROE
10. B X C K G   C Z T O Z K

Lesson 8

Looking for a Job?

Words for Study

advise	actual	vague	talents
alphabetized	experiments	available	survey
parachute	dictates	contact	creating
attitude	grindstone	wallflowers	Judaism

Looking for a Job?

When you're out there looking for a job, the experts will usually advise you to study the newspaper ads daily from *A* to *Z* because ads are often alphabetized according to job title. In an extremely helpful book titled *What Color Is Your Parachute?*, written for people who are hunting for a job or trying to change careers, the author claims that reading the classified ads isn't the only way to go about getting a job. It isn't even the best way.

One of the most important factors in getting the job that is right for you is a right attitude. To have a right attitude, we need to get rid of wrong thinking. The following sections from *What Color Is Your Parachute?* describe what faulty thinking is and how we can replace it with the right attitude toward job-hunting.

Faulty Thinking #1. Many job-hunters believe they don't need to work very hard at the job-hunt. They think they can settle for devoting just a few hours a week to the task of finding employment since "something will always turn up."

Not true! Common sense, as well as actual experiments, show that the harder you work at the job-hunt, the shorter will be the length of your unemployment—other things being equal.

Experience dictates that you can't wait for something to come to you; you must go to it. Moreover, experience dictates that it is easier, by far, to keep your nose to the grindstone with respect to the job-hunt if you seek the support and company of other job-hunters or at least of other friends.

Faulty Thinking #2. Many job-hunters believe they should remain somewhat vague or unclear about what they want to do, so that they are free to take advantage of whatever jobs may be available.

Not so! If you don't state just exactly what you want to do, first of all to yourself, and then to others, you are handing over that decision to others. And others are either going to dodge the decision or else decide that you are able to do only a certain level of work.

Faulty Thinking #3. Many job-hunters believe they shouldn't waste time contacting the organizations or companies which might be interested in them but are not advertising any job openings since the employers have the upper hand in hiring in the first place.

Nonsense! Looking for employment isn't like a high school prom where the job-hunters sit

---

around the edge of the dance floor like shy wallflowers while the employers are whirling around out in the center of the floor leading the dance. In many cases, those employers are stuck with partners who are forever stepping on their toes. As a result, although the employer may seem to have the upper hand, he is often praying that someone will come to his rescue by cutting in. People who cut in are usually pretty good dancers!

Once you have gotten rid of this faulty thinking, you need to keep in mind these keys for right thinking:

Key #1. You must decide that job-hunting will be for you a full-time job (unless you are presently employed, in which case you will still give it every spare hour possible) and that you will use group support in your job-hunting as much as you can.

The more doors you knock on, the more employers you are likely to see. The more employers you see, the more interviews you will have. The more interviews you have, the more job offers you are likely to receive. The more job offers you receive, the more likely it is that one of these will be a job you like the sound of. Thus, you accept that offer, and your job search is successfully concluded.

Key #2. You must decide just exactly what you want to do. You have got to know what it is you

want, or someone is going to sell you a bill of goods somewhere along the line that can do lasting damage to your sense of worth and your proper use of the talents that God gave you.

Key #3. You must decide just exactly where you want to do it through your own research and personal survey. Job-hunters usually begin by thinking there are too few jobs. Actually, it's just the opposite. There are many jobs; but, unless you decide where you want to work and concentrate your energies on that area, you will soon be exhausted. It will be necessary for you to visit the area you want to work in if you do not already live there. In visiting the place where you most want to work, you want to go from one person to another, creating a chain of links in which each contact you see refers you to another person.

Key #4. You must research in depth the companies that interest you and then approach the person or group in each company who has the power to hire you for the job that you have decided you want to do.

The question that bothers almost everyone new to the job-hunt is "Well, I want to see them, but do they want to see me?" In the next lesson, you will learn what advice the author of *What Color Is Your Parachute?* has to offer about what many job-hunters consider a stressful situation—the job interview.

1   **About the Reading.** Six of the statements below disagree with the advice offered in this reading. Rewrite these statements to agree with the advice. Be sure that your rewritten statements include the author's reason for his advice. For the two statements that already agree with the author, leave the lines blank. Study the example before you begin.

1. When looking for a job, don't spend much time because a job will soon come your way.

   When looking for a job, spend as much time as you can because it is likely that the more time you spend, the sooner you will find a job.

2. When looking for a job, you need to realize that you're on your own because other people don't have the time to offer you any support or advice.

   When looking for a job, seek the support and company of other job-hunters or other friends, you need to keep your nose to the grindstone. and

3. When looking for a job, you should be vague about what you want to do because you will lose out on too many opportunities for employment.

When looking for a job, you shouldn't be vague about what you want to do, because if you are vague, you're handing over the decision.

4. When looking for a job, wait for companies to contact you because if they aren't actively looking for new employees, they are happy with those who work for them.

When looking for a job, you should spend your time contacting companies, because employers are stuck with many employees.

5. When looking for a job, you should see as many employers as possible because this will increase your chances of being offered a job you like the sound of.

6. When looking for a job, look everywhere because there aren't many jobs around.

When looking for a job, look in the place where you most want to work, because there are many jobs if you create a chain of links.

7. When looking for a job, talk to many people because they may give you leads to other people who can help you get the job you want.

8. When looking for a job, don't bother to research who in a company has the power to hire you because each company has only one person who does the hiring.

When looking for a job, bother to research who in a company has the power to hire you, because employers want to see you. then you can find who wants to see you,

2 **Jobs.** To match the jobs with the correct descriptions, choose a word from List A and add a word from List B to it to make a compound word. Study the example before you begin. If you have trouble completing the exercise, look up the word in List A in a dictionary.

List A	List B
bee	broker
brake	jack
cow	keeper
floor	maid
lock	man
lumber	man
middle	master
nurse	puncher
✓screen	setter
station	smith
stock	walker
type	✓writer

screenwriter

stockbroker

middleman

stationmaster

locksmith

~~typepuncher~~ *setter*

beekeeper

~~brake~~maid *man*

floorwalker

lumberjack

nurse~~setter~~ *maid*

cow~~man~~ *puncher*

1. This person can often be found in Hollywood writing scripts for movies.

2. This person can often be found on the floor of the New York Stock Exchange buying and selling stocks and other securities.

3. This person is a trader who buys from producers and sells to consumers.

4. This person is in charge of a railroad or bus station.

5. This person makes or repairs locks.

6. This person often works for a newspaper or publishing company setting the type for newspapers or books.

7. This person tends hives and collects honey.

8. This person also works for the railroad assisting the conductor and checking on the operation of the train's brakes.

9. This person works in a department store watching over the salesclerks and assisting the customers.

10. This person works in a forest felling trees and getting the timber to a mill.

11. This woman or girl is employed to take care of children.

12. This person tends cattle and performs many of his duties on horseback.

3

Antonyms. Circle the antonym for the first word in each line. Study the example before you begin.

1. **defeat:** displeasure retreat scandal (victory)
2. **blameless:** convicted (guilty) uneasy worthy
3. **uneven:** irregular (level) ragged scaly
4. **meaningless:** dull favorite (important) wonderful
5. **respectful:** (impolite) outgoing stubborn unaffected
6. **required:** desirable undesirable unnecessary unusual
7. **actual:** commonplace evil (imagined) (unlikely)
8. **regretful:** concerned confused resentful shameless
9. **precise:** cautious (vague) pointless fantastic
10. **ageless:** (old) diseased existing unhealthy
11. **fierce:** (gentle) daring eager unafraid
12. **thrift:** earnings energy talent (wastefulness)

4

The Suffix -ly. Many people claim that it's not what you do that's important—it's how you do it. Words that end in -ly usually tell how something is done or said. Put the letter of the best answer in the blank at the left.

_(d)_ 1. Reaching for the handkerchief in her pocketbook, Mrs. McCarthy exclaimed ____ to the psychiatrist, "Doctor, you don't think I'm having a nervous breakdown, do you?"

(a) formerly (b) pleasantly (c) securely (d) tearfully

_(c)_ 2. "Nonsense, Mrs. McCarthy," advised Dr. Madman ____ . "As I always say, there's nothing like a little crisis now and then to make life a thrill and my wallet fat."

(a) regretfully (b) faithfully (c) cheerfully (d) regularly

_(a)_ 3. "How can you sit there and be so unconcerned when my life is falling apart at the seams, and I don't know which way to turn!" cried Mrs. McCarthy ____ .

(a) bitterly (b) directly (c) doubtfully (d) formally

_(b)_ 4. "My dear lady," stated Dr. Madman ____ , "if you expect me to regard such a slight problem as having no job, no money, no husband, and no roof over your head as a desperate situation, you are talking to the wrong psychiatrist."

(a) fearfully (b) heartlessly (c) loosely (d) squeamishly _(a)_ 5. "Furthermore," the doctor continued _____ , "I'd like to know just how you intend to pay me for my excellent services if you have no paychecks coming in regularly."

(a) coldly   (b) delightfully   (c) gracefully   (d) sweetly

_(b)_ 6. "You know perfectly well that I don't have the courage to express myself in an interview, so just how am I supposed to find a job," shouted Mrs. McCarthy so _____ that the costly paintings on the walls of Dr. Madman's office almost rattled off their hooks.

(a) actually   (b) forcefully   (c) uncertainly   (d) vaguely

_d_ 7. "Well, you certainly don't seem to be having any difficulty expressing yourself well with me," the psychiatrist _____ noted.

(a) equally   (b) generally   (c) thoughtlessly   (d) correctly

_(c)_ 8. Mrs. McCarthy suddenly sat upright on the black leather couch; for it seemed that Dr. Madman had just said something that was very important for her to consider _____ .

(a) emotionally   (b) stupidly   (c) thoroughly   (d) persistently

_(a)_ 9. "Why, you're right! I'm cured! I'm cured!" declared Mrs. McCarthy _____ as she flung her soaked handkerchief into the wastebasket beside the wise doctor's file cabinet.

(a) joyfully   (b) delicately   (c) privately   (d) uneasily

_(b)_ 10. "Just don't forget to send me $75 from your first paycheck," grinned Dr. Madman as he _____ walked Mrs. McCarthy to the door.

(a) magically   (b) politely   (c) shamefully   (d) questioningly

5   **More Work with the Suffix -ly.** To add -ly to these words, change the y to i and add -ly. Study the example before you begin.

1. angry	_angrily_	7. steady	_steadily_
2. hearty	_heartily_	8. crazy	_crazily_
3. merry	_merrily_	9. dreamy	_dreamily_
4. cheery	_cheerily_	10. unworthy	_unworthily_
5. mighty	_mightily_	11. guilty	_guiltily_
6. worthy	_worthily_	12. moody	_moodily_

6 **Capitalization Rules: Part 3.** Don't feel distressed. You have only four more capitalization rules to learn now. After you have studied these new rules, capitalize the words in the sentences correctly. Remember that the number after each sentence tells you how many words need to be capitalized. Don't forget to apply all the rules for capitalization that you have studied.

11. **Capitalize the first word and all important words in titles of books, plays, movies, TV shows, magazines, newspapers, stories, poems, works of art, and pieces of music**.

    Examples: books . . . . Gone with the Wind
    plays . . . . The Man Who Came to Dinner
    movies . . . . The Sound of Music
    TV shows . . . . The Price Is Right
    magazines . . . . Time, TV Guide, Field and Stream
    newspapers . . . . New York Daily News
    stories . . . . We're the Only Colored People Here
    poems . . . . Stopping by Woods on a Snowy Evening
    works of art . . . . Last Supper, The Thinker
    pieces of music . . . . How Deep Is the Ocean?

12. **Capitalize names referring to the one God of a religion, religions and their followers, and major religious writings**.

    Examples: the one God of a religion . . . . God, Lord, Messiah, Buddha, Allah
    religions . . . . Christianity, Judaism, Islam
    followers of religions . . . . Baptists, Mormons, Catholics, Jews
    religious writings . . . . Bible, Koran, Talmud, the Old Testament, the Book of Job

    Note: Do not capitalize the word *god* when it is used to refer to a religion with many gods.
    Example: The Greek god Pan watched over flocks, fields, and forests.

13. **Capitalize course names followed by a number and language courses**.
    Examples: Math 153, History 101, Italian

    Note: Do not capitalize the names of school subjects.
    Examples: history, reading, art

14. **Capitalize East, West, North, and South when they refer to recognized sections of the country or of the world**.
    Examples: the South, the Middle East

    Note: Do not capitalize these words when they tell directions.

    Examples: Many geese head south for the winter.
    Colorado is west of Illinois.

1. in english class on thursday, the students groaned when mr. fisher told them they would have to have completed reading *a tale of two cities* by monday. (10)

2. while traveling through the south, the trentons stopped at the stony brook motel, which was located on the east end of beech avenue in memphis. (9)

3. francis scott key wrote "the star-spangled banner" during the war of 1812 while he was a prisoner on a british warship. (9)

4. when peggy won the fishing contest sponsored by hickock county, her picture appeared in the *grand island daily times*. (8)

5. mrs. ritz wrote a letter to the department of transportation in washington, d.c., to complain about the condition of the highways in parts of new england. (9)

6. upon reading his application for smothers business college, louise asked mick, "just tell me why you plan to enroll in typing II when you nearly flunked typing I last year at walnut hills high school." (13)

7. mr. east drove north five blocks along north street when he should have driven south five blocks along south street, so he completely missed his interview with the manager of west branch savings & loan. (10)

8. when jesse took a religion course in college, he studied christianity, judaism, and islam by reading selections from the bible, the talmud, and the koran. (8)

9. the american red cross and the sons of italy combined their efforts to offer relief to the flood victims by opening a shelter in the basement of moosewood city hall. (9)

10. leafing through the pages of *family circle* magazine, june jefferson noticed an unusual recipe for boston cream pie which she considered making for the helping hand club's autumn bake sale. (9)

7 **A Skills Survey.** The author of *What Color Is Your Parachute*? believes that, generally speaking, all skills can be separated into six groups. To see which ones you enjoy using, try this exercise.

Below is a view of a room in which a party is taking place. At this party, people with the same or nearly the same interests have all joined one another in the same corner of the room as described below:

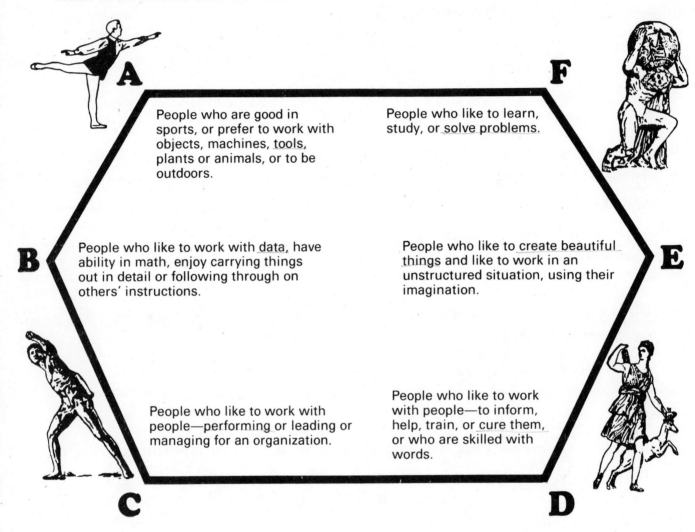

A — People who are good in sports, or prefer to work with objects, machines, tools, plants or animals, or to be outdoors.

F — People who like to learn, study, or solve problems.

B — People who like to work with data, have ability in math, enjoy carrying things out in detail or following through on others' instructions.

E — People who like to create beautiful things and like to work in an unstructured situation, using their imagination.

C — People who like to work with people—performing or leading or managing for an organization.

D — People who like to work with people—to inform, help, train, or cure them, or who are skilled with words.

1. Which corner of the room would you go to first because in it is the group of people you would most enjoy being with for the longest time? (Put aside any questions you might have about shyness or whether you will have to talk to them.) Write the letter for that corner here: _A_

2. After fifteen minutes, everyone in the corner you have chosen leaves for another party except you. Of the groups that still remain, which corner would you now be drawn to the most? Write the letter for that corner here: _B_

3. After fifteen minutes, this group also leaves for another party. You're still there, however. Of the groups that remain, which one would you most enjoy being with for the longest time? Write the letter for that corner here: _D_

4. Now underline the skills in each corner that you like best.

5. Based on your skills survey, describe the type of job that interests you the most. Be sure to include details in your description.

   I was a computer engineer in Japan, and like to make something with tools. The type of job that interests me the most is A. I would like to be skillful.

Lesson 9

The Job Interview

Words for Study

realistic	circumstances	positive	minor
individual	salary	social	immediate
quality	occupation	signature	major
volunteer	benefits	felony	previous
negative	guarantee	omission	graduate

The Job Interview

To prepare yourself for a job interview, you most certainly want to pay attention to your appearance. Studies have shown that neatness pays off in the job hunt. Do remember to look like you deserve the job. Wear a good-looking outfit. Have a decent haircut, clean fingernails, clean breath, and shined shoes. It may seem like a silly game to you, but it's a game with very high stakes in which you want to be the winner.

As the interview gets under way, you can, of course, try to figure out what is going on in the mind of that person sitting on the other side of the desk. This is not realistic. If you want to take the more realistic view, just imagine that every interviewer is a complete individual in his or her own right—just as you are. You don't know anything about that interviewer except that he probably has problems which, he hopes, you will help solve.

Use the interview to discover what the interviewer thinks those problems are. Remember, the main thing you want to get across during the interview is to show how your skills can help his company solve their problems. Just be sure you're talking about *their* ideas about the problems that confront their business or organization and not *your* ideas.

For example, let's say you're interviewing for a job in a machine shop. The person doing the hiring is convinced that his main problem is not enough workers. Your concept of the machine shop's main problem, however, is that the machinery is outdated. If you need help figuring out what's going to happen if you start talking about the poor quality of the machinery right off the bat, just imagine how you'd feel if a total stranger came into your living room one evening and started telling you how to live your life!

In addition to *never* telling the interviewer how to run his business, there are two more *never's* to keep in mind. One: *never* volunteer negative information about yourself. Whatever the interviewer may ask about your past (like, why did you leave your last job?), remember the only thing he is actually interested in is the future (under what circumstances might you leave me?). Two: *never* accept or reject a job offer on the spot. Feel free to say to the interviewer if he's just offered you a position, "I need some time to consider this."

Finally—a woman was once describing her very first job to me. It was at a soda fountain. I asked her what her biggest surprise at that job was. "My first paycheck," she said. "I know it sounds funny, but I was so green at all this that during the entire interview for the job, it never occurred to me to ask what my salary would be. I just took it for granted that it would be a fair salary. Did I ever get a shock when my first paycheck came! It was so small that I could

---

hardly believe it. Did I ever learn a lesson from that!"

Yes, and so may we all. It is a good idea to do a little research on salaries before your interview. Why? First of all, remember that the only proper place for a discussion about salary is at the end of the job interview. Let's say the interviewer likes you, and you like the idea of working for the company or organization. Then, the interviewer says, "How much salary were you expecting?"

This brings us to the second and more important point. If you have done a little research and know the salary ranges for the job for which you're applying, you can name a figure near or at the top of the range. But suppose you didn't do your research. Then you're up a creek without a paddle, as they say. You will be surprised at how much information you can find about salaries in books available at your library. If the library can't help you, remember that almost every occupation has its own group whose business it is to keep tabs on what is happening with salaries within that occupation or field.

In your discussion about salary, do not forget to pay attention to "fringe benefits." In a recent year, it was found that such "fringes" as life insurance, health benefits, vacation or holiday plans, and retirement programs can add up to 25% of a worker's salary. Also, don't forget that salary discussions during the hiring interview are more than just a matter of agreeing upon a starting salary. The question: "When and under what circumstances can I expect to have my salary raised?" needs not only to be asked, but also to be put in writing. The road to hell is paved with promises that are unwritten and which employers often forget once you are hired.

There is an old saying: "Give me a fish, and I will eat for today. Teach me to fish, and I will eat for the rest of my life." The suggestions you have just read from *What Color Is Your Parachute*? are an effort to teach you how to fish with respect to one of the most difficult tasks any of us faces in life: the job hunt. Do these suggestions always work? Of course not. This is job-hunting, not magic. No one can fully guarantee you a job exactly where you want it, doing exactly what you want, at the salary you desire. But many people who have followed these suggestions—who have learned how to fish—get very close, and some succeed completely.

1 **About the Reading.** Put the letter of the correct answer on the line to the left.

(c) 1. The proper time to discuss salary with the person doing the hiring is ____ .
   (a) after you've been hired
   (b) at the beginning of the interview
   (c) at the end of the interview
   (d) never

(d) 2. When the woman describing her first job remarked, "...but I was so green at all this..." she means ____ .
   (a) she felt too ill at the time of the interview to ask about wages
   (b) she felt too terrified to ask how much she would be paid
   (c) she needed work so badly that, at first, the size of her paycheck didn't concern her
   (d) she was too new at working to realize that she should have asked about her wages during the interview

_(a)_   3. If you had a negative experience at your previous place of employment, you should avoid ____ during the interview.

    (a) volunteering this information
    (b) speaking honestly about this experience
    (c) thinking about the past
    (d) discussing any details of your former job

_(d)_   4. When discussing the problems faced by the company for which you're considering working, you should ____ .

    (a) comfort the interviewer with such remarks as, "I'm sure everything will work out all right in the long run."
    (b) realize that, as an outsider, you can see their problems clearly and offer all the advice you can
    (c) realize that, as an outsider, you have no right to say anything
    (d) strive to understand the problems from their point of view

_(b)_   5. To be "up a creek without a paddle" means you've gotten yourself into a(n) ____ situation.

    (a) adventurous   (b) dangerous   (c) helpless   (d) worthless

_(c)_   6. Which of the following is not listed as a "fringe benefit"? .

    (a) holidays   (b) insurance   (c) medical plans   (d) salary increases

_(c)_   7. Which common saying means about the same thing as "Give me a fish, and I will eat for today. Teach me to fish, and I will eat for the rest of my life."?

    (a) "A bird in the hand is worth two in the bush."
    (b) "A stitch in time saves nine." （今日の一針 あすの十針）
    (c) "God helps those who help themselves."
    (d) "Hitch your wagon to a star." ?

_(a)_   8. The author of *What Color Is Your Parachute?* ____ .

    (a) offers his assistance to those who are looking for employment
    (b) realizes that finding the right job is a matter of luck
    (c) thinks that following his suggestions guarantees a good job
    (d) believes there is no available information to assist the job-hunter .

2 **Positive and Negative.** In every situation with which we're confronted we can respond in either a positive or negative way. Read the situations listed below and then give an example of both a positive and a negative response. Study the example before you begin.

1. *Situation*: The bus on which you're riding to your job interview has just broken down, and you realize that you can't make it to the interview on time.

    Positive: Get to a telephone as quickly as possible, explain the circumstances to the interviewer, and request another appointment.

    Negative: Think "Well, that's the story of my life," sit back, and feel sorry for yourself while the bus is being repaired.

2. *Situation*: It is the morning of an important job interview, and you are deciding what to wear.

   Positive: _I'll wear a good-looking outfit because I want to get the job._

   Negative: _I don't care about my outfit, because it doesn't effect the job hunt_

3. *Situation*: At the beginning of the job interview, the interviewer asks you to describe what skills you have to offer.

   Positive: _I'll think what skill is needed for the company or organization, and tell my best ability._

   Negative: _I don't tell my ability very much if the interviewer isn't interested in it._

4. *Situation*: At the end of the job interview, the interviewer tells you that he or she is very interested in hiring you and wants to know what kind of salary you're expecting.

   Positive: _I know the avarage of this job, and I can tell how much is proper for me._

   Negative: _I can't tell how much I should get, and so I'll obey the company._

5. *Situation*: You learn that someone else was hired for the job you were hoping to get.

   Positive: _I'll call the company, and tell that I would like an interview again._

   Negative: _The job hunt at the company was finished, and I'll not contact it anymore._

3

How Would You Classify This? Choose the word in the row that is the best classification for the first word and write it on the line to the right. Study the example before you begin.

1. **Alabama:**	city	state	nation	the South	*state*
2. **tractor:**	tool	machinery	grindstone	possession	*machinery*
3. **salary:**	outcome	expense	income	benefits	*income*
4. **prom:**	chore	merriment	engagement	social event	*social event*
5. **taxi:**	risk	carfare	adventure	transportation	*transportation*
6. **foreman:** 職長	protector	supervisor	salesman	officeholder 公務員	*supervisor*
7. **guarantee:**	promise	signature	experiment	preference	*promise*
8. **felony:** [félǝni] 重罪	crime	attitude	omission 省略	punishment	*crime*
9. **millimeter:**	depth	celluloid	projector	measurement	*measurement*
10. **wristwatch:**	present	costume	timepiece	timecard	*timepiece*
11. **fury:** 激怒	thought	emotion	occupation	circumstance	*emotion*
12. **Uncle Sam:**	symbol	country	fighter	employer	*symbol*

4

More Work with Classifications. Enter the following abbreviations under the correct classification on the chart below. Don't forget the necesssary periods. Study the example before you begin.

✓AL	Fr.	Jap.	NY	Sat.
Aug.	Fri.	lb.	oz.	Sept.
CA	gal.	MA	pt.	Thurs.
Dec.	Ital.	Mar.	qt.	WA
Eng.	Jan.	Mon.	Rus.	Wed.

Days of the Week	Languages	Measurements	U.S. States	Months of the Year
Fri.	Eng.	gal.	AL	Aug.
Mon.	Fr.	lb.	CA	Dec.
Sat.	Ital.	oz.	MA	Jan.
Thurs.	Jap.	pt. ②	NY	Mar.
Wed.	Rus.	qt.	WA	Sept.

5 **More Work with the Suffix -ly.** Choose the word that correctly completes each sentence and write it in the blank. Study the example before you begin.

legal
legally

1. The landlady wondered whether or not she was ___legally___ responsible as she surveyed the minor water damage in the first-floor apartment.

positive
positively

2. Eddie was ___positive___ that after doing such a fine job mowing Mrs. Clark's lawn he would be given referrals for other jobs.

immediate
immediately

3. Ginger's ___immediate___ availability was one reason she landed the job as a computer operator which she read about in the classified advertisements in the Sunday paper.

fearless
fearlessly

4. "I'm no coward," the knight declared ___fearlessly___ as he rushed to the rescue of the fair, young princess in distress.

current
currently

5. "The prisoner's file is ___currently___ under review, and I should have an answer to your question by early next week," replied the warden in response to the lawyer's question.

useless
uselessly

6. "It's ___useless___ for me to try to talk some sense into you," moaned the manager. "Since you're the owner of the team, you're going to do things the way you want to in spite of my excellent advice."

popular
popularly

7. James B. Hickok was ___popularly___ known as "Wild Bill" to friends and enemies alike in the Old West.

separate
separately

8. When he requested ___separate___ checks, Margaret's handsome date brought a sad, sad end to what had been a most delightful evening.

impolite
impolitely

9. "Now, Jerome, you know it's ___impolite___ to eat with your fingers," the babysitter reminded the eleven-year-old who had just stuck his thumb into a meatball and was eating it as if it were a lollipop.

useful
usefully

10. So she would still feel ___useful___ now that her four children were grown and married, Mrs. Plumber devoted her time to volunteering her skills at the day-care center.

social
socially

11. Phyllis was such a ___social___ butterfly that she considered her

week a disaster if every single evening wasn't filled with some exciting

engagement.

negative
negatively

12. "I'm not speaking ___negatively___; I'm just being realistic," stated the

barber who predicted that few customers would cross his doorway that Friday

because of the eight-inch snowstorm the night before.

individual
individually

13. Martin surrounded his birthday cake with ___individually___-wrapped gifts

for every guest he had invited to celebrate his fortieth birthday—a major

event in his mind.

previous
previously

14. Gail was ___previously___ earning less than she is in her new job, which

she found after earning her typing certificate.

realistic
realistically

15. "You can't ___realistically___ expect me to keep this silly curfew *every*

weekend!" Dan's teenage daughter complained.

6 **Filling out an Employment Application.** For most jobs, you need to fill out an
application before you are even granted an interview. To give you some practice at
this, fill out the employment application on the next two pages. Some of the words
may be new to you, but if you sound them out according to rules you have studied
previously, you should have no trouble.

EMPLOYMENT APPLICATION

Name _Yukiko Aoyama_   Date _Mar. 12. 2001_

Home Phone

Address _13802 ROSEBRANCH CT._   Social Security Number _N/A_

City _HOUSTON_   State _TX_ Zip _77059_

Position Applied for: _____   Date Available _____

Do you wish to work: _✓_ Full time? ____ Part time?   U.S. Citizen? _No_

Education:

	Name of school	Address of school	Dates From	To	Did you Graduate?	Course or Degree
High School	Toho High School	Japan			Yes	
College or University	Tokai University	Japan			Yes	Aeronautics and Astronautics
Business or Trade School						
Other						

Employment History: List current employment first. Include any military service.

1.

Employer Telephone	Dates Employed From	To	Work Performed
Nippon Electric Company			
Address			
Japan	1987	1998	
Job Title	Hourly rate/Salary Starting	Final	
System Engineer			
Immediate Supervisor			
Mr. Tomoyuki Ichikawa	¥150,000	¥350,000	
Reason for Leaving	/MONTH	/MONTH	
Moving to the U.S.A.			

2.

Employer Telephone	Dates Employed From	To	Work Performed
Address			
Job Title	Hourly rate/Salary Starting	Final	
Immediate Supervisor			
Reason for Leaving			

Personal:

Organizations, hobbies, interests, or other activities (Exclude activities which indicate race, religion, or national origin).

I'm interested in computers, and my hobby is traveling.

_____

_____

_____

Have you previously worked for this company? *No.*

If yes: Dates employed: from _____ to _____ Position: _____

Were you ever convicted of a felony? *No.* If yes, give details _____

Job Related Skills:

Please indicate those areas in which you have had previous experience or training:

_____ Management	_✓_ Computer operator	_____ Repairs
_____ Sales	_____ Typing	_____ Stockroom
_____ Customer service	_____ Bookkeeping	_____ Cleaning
_____ Cash register	_____ Shorthand	_____ Other _____

Medical: (If hired you may be required to take a physical exam.)

Do you have a disability that might prevent you from doing the job that you are applying for? *No.*

If yes, explain. _____

References: (Not employers or relatives)

Name and Address	Occupation	Phone

Please Read Carefully:

I hereby state that these answers are correct and complete to the best of my knowledge and belief, and hereby permit the company to investigate any of the information contained herein concerning my personal character, habits or employment records. I understand that if I am hired, any false statement or omission of facts contained herein will be cause for my immediate dismissal.

Signature: _____ 堂小友己子 _____ Date: _Mar, 12, 2001_

An Equal Opportunity Employer

Lesson 10

How to Avoid a Job

Words for Study

solution	marbles	resumed	innocent
whitewash	pure	reckon	soldier
spirit	inspiration	Polly	couple
multiplied	scorn	particular	tadpoles
examined	artist	barrel	idle

How to Avoid a Job

Sometimes, as we all know, we just don't feel like working. In the passage below from Mark Twain's story *The Adventures of Tom Sawyer*, Tom hits upon a solution to this well-known problem.

* * *

Saturday morning was come, and all the summer world was bright and fresh and brimming with life. There was a song in every heart and cheer in every face. Tom appeared on the sidewalk with a bucket of whitewash and a long-handled brush. He surveyed the fence, and all gladness left him and a deep sadness settled down upon his spirit. Thirty yards of board nine feet high! Life to him seemed hollow and a burden.

Sighing, he dipped his brush and passed it along the topmost plank; repeated the operation; did it again; compared the white-washed streak with the vastness of unwhitewashed fence, and sat down on a box discouraged. He began to think of the fun he had planned for the day, and his sorrows multiplied. Soon, the free boys would come along, and they would make a world of fun of him for having to work—the very thought of it burnt him like fire. He got out his worldly wealth from his pocket and examined it—bits of toys, marbles, and trash; enough to buy an exchange of work maybe, but not half enough to buy so much as half an hour of pure freedom. So he gave up the idea of trying to buy the boys.

At this dark and hopeless moment, an inspiration burst upon him! Nothing less than a great, wonderful inspiration.

He took up his brush and went calmly to work. Ben Rogers came into sight presently—the very boy, of all boys, whose scorn he had been dreading. Ben was eating an apple and as he drew near, he slowed down and took to the middle of the street, playing a game in which he pretended he was a steamboat.

Tom went on whitewashing—paid no attention to the steamboat. Ben stared a moment and then said: "Hi! You're up a stump, ain't you!"

No answer. Tom surveyed his last touch with the eye of an artist; then gave his brush another gentle sweep and surveyed the result, as before. Ben ranged up alongside of him. Tom's mouth watered for the apple, but he stuck to his work.

Ben said, "Hello, old chap, you got to work, hey?"

Tom wheeled suddenly and said, "Why it's you, Ben! I warn't noticing."

"Say—I'm going in a-swimming, I am. Don't you wish you could? But of course you'd druther work—wouldn't you? Course you would!"

Tom studied the boy a bit and said, "What do you call work?"

"Why, ain't *that* work?"

Tom resumed his whitewashing and answered carelessly, "Well, maybe it is, and maybe it ain't. All I know is it suits Tom Sawyer."

"Oh, come now, you don't mean to let on that you *like* it?"

The brush continued to move.

Presently Ben said, "Say, Tom, let me whitewash a little."

Tom considered, was about to consent, but he altered his mind. "No—no—I reckon it wouldn't hardly do, Ben. You see, Aunt Polly's awful particular about this fence—right here on the street, you know—but if it was the back fence I wouldn't mind and *she* wouldn't. Yes, she's awful particular about this fence; it's got to be done very careful; I reckon there ain't one boy in a thousand, maybe two thousand, that can do it the way it's got to be done."

"Oh, shucks, I'll be just as careful. Now lemme try. Say—I'll give you the core of my apple. I'll give you *all* of it!"

Tom gave up the brush with unwillingness written on his face, but with joy in his heart. And while Ben worked and sweated in the sun, the retired artist sat on a barrel in the shade close by, munched on his apple and planned the slaughter of more innocent boys. There was no lack of victims; boys happened along every little while; they came to jeer, but remained to whitewash. By the time Ben was tired, Tom had traded the next chance to Billy Fisher for a kite. And so on and so on, hour after hour.

When the middle of the afternoon came, Tom was rolling in wealth. For granting the honor of whitewashing, Tom had received in return twelve marbles, part of a jew's-harp, a piece of blue glass to look through, a key that wouldn't unlock anything, a piece of chalk, a tin soldier, a couple of tadpoles, six firecrackers, a kitten with only one eye, a brass doorknob, the handle of a knife, and four pieces of orange peel.

He had had a nice, good, idle time all the while—plenty of company—and the fence had three coats of whitewash on it! Tom said to himself that it was not such a hollow world, after all. He had discovered a great law of human action without knowing it—namely, that in order to make a man or a boy want something badly, it is only necessary to make the thing difficult to get. If he had been a great and wise man, he would have now understood that Work consists of what a body *has* to do, and that Play consists of whatever a body doesn't have to do.

Adapted from the *Mark Twain Reader*. Courtesy of W. H. Smith Publishers, Inc.

1   **About the Story.** Answer the following questions in good sentence form.

1. At the beginning of the story, why does life seem "hollow and a burden" to Tom?

     Because he had to paint thirty yards of board nine feet high, but he didn't want to do that.

2. At the end of the story, why does Tom say to himself that the world is not so hollow after all?

     He made other boys work his job, and could get many things.

3. Why was it probably a good thing for Tom that the first boy who came along was the boy "whose scorn he had been dreading"?

     The boy had scorned Tom's work, and Tom pretended that his work was too difficult for the boy. Tom made the boy want to do that.

4. Why doesn't Tom let Ben whitewash the fence immediately after Ben says he'd like to try it?

     Tom tries to make the work difficult to get, and that makes Ben want the work badly.

5. What is the "law of human action" that Tom has used, without even realizing it, to get the boys to whitewash the fence for him? _i.e. The harder it is to get something, the more you want it._

     It's that in order to make a man or a boy want something badly, it is only necessary to make the things difficult to get.

6. According to Mark Twain, what is the difference between work and play?

     Work consists of what a boy has to do, and play consists of whatever a boy doesn't have to do.

7. Give an example of something that is work to you but might be considered play by someone else. Explain your reason for choosing this particular example.

     Mixing to make cakes is the work for me, but it's the play for my niece. She wants to handle the mixer.

8. Give an example of something that is play to you but might be considered work by someone else. Explain your reason for choosing this particular example.

     Walking out is the play for me, but it's the work for my husband. Because he has to loose his weight.

2 **If Only Someone Else Would Do It!** Unlike Tom Sawyer, most workers can't go around tricking other people into doing their jobs. But if they could... Match the workers with the statements they might make to snare an innocent listener into taking their job for a day.

butcher
cowpuncher
dressmaker
floorwalker
lifeguard
scribe (書記者)
stationmaster
student
teacher
treasurer (会計係)

dressmaker 1. "Creating new patterns and ripping out seams is such a breeze that it's like being paid for relaxing."

student 2. "Doing homework is much more inspiring than hanging out with friends every evening."

teacher 3. "Grading homework is so much less demanding than doing it, and it's such a rewarding way to spend one's time."

floorwalker 4. "Nabbing shoplifters makes me feel just as brave and brainy as all those detectives you see on television."

stationmaster 5. "Nothing ever really bothers me because I know if things start to get frantic, I can always escape on the next train."

butcher 6. "Quartering these steers gives me all the muscles, money, and merriment that a man could ever hope for in life."

lifeguard 7. "Rescuing little children, getting a beautiful tan, flirting—that pretty well describes my ideal job."

treasurer 8. "The greatest thing about handling the company's money all day is that I can pretend that it's mine and that I am rich."

cowpuncher 9. "Riding herd on the range all day gives a body freedom and that feeling of being out where no boss can roam."

scribe 10. "Writing love letters for other people is far more exciting and less troublesome than actually being in love yourself."

Of these ten statements, which one sounds like the best deal to you?

Student.

Which one sounds like the worst?

Butcher.

3 **Word Relationships.** On the line at the left, write the letter of the answer that best completes each statement. Study the example before you begin.

___b___ 1. Image is to sight as _____ .

   (a) dialogue is to touch   (c) scene is to sound
   (b) food is to taste   (d) stuffy nose is to smell

___b___ 2. Major is to minor as _____ .

   (a) blameless is to innocent   (c) insecure is to worried
   (b) graduate is to enroll   (d) vast is to immense

___a___ 3. Hollywood is to the movie industry as _____ .

   (a) Detroit is to the automobile industry
   (b) New York City is to the United Nations
   (c) Oklahoma is to the oil industry
   (d) Tennessee is to the record business

___a C___ 4. Examine is to investigate as _____ .

   (a) indicate is to reckon   (c) benefit is to aid
   (b) dictate is to advise   (d) resume is to dismiss

___d___ 5. White is to wedding as _____ .

   (a) red is to wine   (c) blue is to ocean
   (b) green is to grass   (d) black is to funeral

___d___ 6. Italy is to Europe as _____ .

   (a) Egypt is to Asia   (c) Mexico is to South America
   (b) Spain is to Africa   (d) Canada is to North America

___b___ 7. Millimeter is to film as _____ .

   (a) ounce is to diamond   (c) movie is to projector
   (b) caliber is to bullet   (d) revolver is to gun

___c___ 8. Medical knowledge is to physician as _____ .

   (a) future is to ancestor   (c) law is to judge
   (b) diet is to weightlifter   (d) wallop is to gunfighter

___d___ 9. Busybody is to nosiness as _____ .

   (a) consumer is to grouchiness
   (b) hitchhiker is to fussiness
   (c) volunteer is to unwillingness
   (d) wallflower is to shyness

___a___ 10. Vaguely is to precisely as _____ .

   (a) cheerily is to moodily
   (b) immediately is to promptly
   (c) positively is to certainly
   (d) regretfully is to sorrowfully

4 **Review of Suffixes.** Add one of the suffixes listed in the box to the underlined word in each sentence so that the sentences make sense. When adding a suffix, you may need to drop or change some letters. Study the example before you begin.

-ful   -less   -ly   -ment   -ness

judgment

1. When the shortstop was thrown out of the game, he shouted at the umpire, "Your judge_____ is as lousy as your eyesight!"

contentment

2. After a roast beef dinner and two servings of chocolate fudge cake, Grandfather lay down for his Sunday afternoon nap with a look of perfect content_____ on his face.

merciless

3. Although all wars could be described as senseless, World War II has been called "the most mercy_____ of all the wars."

blankness

4. Kenneth could tell by the blank_____ of his girlfriend's expression that she wasn't listening to a word he said.

vastly

5. "I'm delighted to report," said the nurse to the worried parents, "that your daughter's condition has vast_____ improved, and she will probably be moved to the children's ward after the doctor checks her chart."

purely

6. It was pure_____ by accident, the young lovers thought, that fog had grounded the plane thus giving them a few more wonderful hours to spend with each other.

scornful

7. Mrs. Olson's arguments always turned into out-and-out battles because when she cast scorn_____ looks at all those who happened to disagree with her, they felt as if they had to defend their lives as well as their viewpoints.

vagueness

8. Patty's tone of voice sounded innocent enough, but her mother knew from the vague_____ of her answers that she had been doing something she shouldn't have.

merciful

9. "Please be mercy_____ with this poor young man," pleaded the lawyer before the jury. "If you convict him, it is you who will be guilty of committing a crime."

dutiful

10. Rob tried to be a duty_____ son, but it seemed as if his parents expected more of him than he was able to give.

bareness

11. Upon entering the two-room apartment, the caseworker immediately realized from the bare_____ of the front room that the family truly needed help.

innocently　12. "We didn't do it, ma'am," declared the leader of the gang <u>innocent</u>
when the policewoman demanded to know who had picked all the prize-
winning roses in Mr. Frank's garden.

limitless　13. When Mr. Campbell heard that job opportunities in Alaska were
<u>limit</u>, he decided he'd give moving there a try even though he wasn't
particularly fond of freezing temperatures.

childless　14. When the interviewer asked the couple how many children they had, Kirk
shook his head and said sorrowfully, "None. My wife and I are <u>child</u>."

misjudgement　15. "Your <u>misjudge</u> in this real estate deal has cost our firm thousands of
dollars and you, your job. You're fired!" shrieked Ms. Shark to the
shaking employee.

5 **Spelling.** Below are statements made by Mark Twain in some of his other books. One of the underlined words in each statement is misspelled. Rewrite the misspelled word correctly on the line.

differences   1. One of the most <u>striking</u> <u>diffrences</u> between a cat and a lie is that a cat has <u>only</u> nine <u>lives</u>.

lightning   2. <u>Thunder</u> is good, it makes an <u>impression</u>: but it is <u>lightening</u> that <u>does</u> the work.

possession   3. Each <u>person</u> is born to one <u>posession</u> which outvalues all his <u>others</u>—his last <u>breath</u>.

somebody   4. <u>Sorrow</u> can take care of <u>itself</u>, but to get the full <u>value</u> of a joy, you must have <u>sombody</u> to share it with.

your   5. "<u>Behold</u>," the fool says, "Put not all <u>you're</u> eggs in one basket," but the wise man says, "Put all <u>your</u> eggs in one basket and <u>WATCH</u> THAT BASKET."

starving   6. If you pick up a <u>starveing</u> dog and make him <u>wealthy</u>, he will not bite you. This is the main <u>difference</u> <u>between</u> a dog and a man.

hundred   7. <u>April</u> 1. This is the day upon <u>which</u> we are reminded of what we are on the other three <u>hunderd</u> and <u>sixty-four</u>.

cabbage   8. He is <u>useless</u> on top of the ground; he <u>ought</u> to be under it, <u>inspiring</u> <u>cabages</u>.

cannot   9. It is <u>often</u> the case that the man who <u>cant</u> tell a <u>lie</u> thinks he is the best <u>judge</u> of one.

promise   10. To <u>promis</u> not to do a thing is the <u>surest</u> way in the world to make a <u>body</u> want to go and do that <u>very</u> thing.

thankful   11. Let us be <u>thankfull</u> for the <u>fools</u>. But for them the rest of us <u>could</u> not <u>succeed</u>.

experience   12. We should be <u>careful</u> to get out of an <u>expereince</u> only the <u>wisdom</u> that is in it—and stop there; lest we be like the cat that sits down on a hot stove lid. She will never sit down on a hot stove lid again—and that is well; but also she will never sit down on a cold one <u>anymore</u>.

6   **What Exactly Is a Jew's-Harp?** To learn more about this instrument, choose the correct word for each of the blanks in this description.

Asia	create	Europe	glory	popular
concerts	damaged	finger	incorrectly	resume
consists	dentist	gentlemen	instrument	traveled

The Jew's-Harp

A jew's-harp is not a harp. Neither is it, as some people _incorrectly_ believe, a Jewish instrument. The jew's-harp is a small, musical instrument. It _consists_ of a curved metal frame with a metal strip connected to one end. The other end of the strip is slimmer and bent forward. Players hold the metal frame against their teeth and _create_ musical notes by striking the metal strip with the _finger_ .

Sometimes there are risks. In the early 1800s, for example, one performer who _traveled_ throughout Europe giving _concerts_ on the jew's-harp had teeth that were so badly _damaged_ by the iron instrument that he was in great pain every time he performed. He decided he had to start playing another instrument. But then, he found a _dentist_ who agreed to construct a cover for his teeth. Using this cover, the performer was able to _resume_ playing his favorite _instrument_.

The jew's-harp has been played in Asia since the 1100s and in _Europe_ since the 1300s. After a brief moment of _glory_ in the early 1800s, the jew's-harp was replaced by the increasingly popular mouth organ. Currently, jew's-harp playing is _popular_ in folk music and with children in the United States. And in _Asia_ , ladies are still courted by _gentlemen_ playing quiet and romantic songs on this instrument.

Review: Lessons 1-10

1   **Word Review.** Use the words listed below to fill in the blanks correctly. Don't forget to capitalize when necessary.

Abraham Lincoln	felony (重罪) [félonī]	roll call
applicant	interview	suffix
crisis (危機)	Mark Twain	United Nations
experiment	prefix	whitewash

interview   1.   a face-to-face meeting for the formal discussion of some matter; a talk between a reporter and a person from whom he seeks facts or statements

suffix   2.   a letter or letters added to the end of a word to alter its meaning or form a new word

prefix   3.   a letter or letters put before a word, which alters its meaning

whitewash   4.   a mixture of lime and water, often with glue added, that is used to whiten walls, concrete, etc.

crisis   5.   a serious condition in which a sudden or meaningful change seems about to occur; an extremely important moment or situation; a turning point

experiment   6.   a test made to decide the value of something previously untried, prove a known truth, or examine an idea

Mark Twain   7.   American author (1835–1910) who wrote *The Adventures of Tom Sawyer*

United Nations   8.   an organization of countries with headquarters in New York City which was founded in 1945 to promote world peace and security

felony   9.   any of several crimes such as murder, rape, or burglary which can result in strict punishment

applicant   10.   one who applies for something, such as a job

roll call   11.   the reading aloud of a list of names of people, as in a classroom or military post, to see who is absent

Abraham Lincoln   12.   sixteenth president of the United States who served as president during the War Between the States (1861–1865)

2 **Word Review.** Write the word that could best replace each underlined word or phrase in the blank on the left.

_____(d)_____ 1. After a long discussion, the employees at the travel agency decided upon a <u>stagecoach</u> for their <u>sign</u> because it suggested trips filled with adventure and excitement.

   (a) application   (b) judgment   (c) quality   (d) symbol

_____(c)_____ 2. After the interview, Ralph had the <u>feeling</u> that he should have said more about his previous job experience.

   (a) admission   (b) commission   (c) impression   (d) omission

_____(a)_____ 3. "Don't worry," said Dr. Ruby, "a few <u>slight</u> adjustments, and your back will feel just fine again."

   (a) minor   (b) major   (c) pure   (d) unpleasant

_____(d)_____ 4. Francis <u>turned up his nose at</u> the salary offer because he thought he was worth far more than the petty sum the interviewer had just quoted.

   (a) adjusted   (b) preferred   (c) reckoned   (d) scorned

_____(d)_____ 5. From sunrise to sunset, Peggy preferred to have every moment of her day completely planned because <u>idle</u> periods of time always made her feel uneasy and tense.

   (a) undesirable   (b) unstructured   (c) unusual   (d) unworthy

_____(b)_____ 6. The chairman argued that Hiram should be put in charge of the fund-raising drive because he was <u>somebody you could always count on</u> when it came to hard work.

   (a) available   (b) dependable   (c) forceful   (d) realistic

_____(a)_____ 7. The commander inspired such <u>intense</u> loyalty among his troops that they probably would have followed him anywhere.

   (a) fierce   (b) individual   (c) lifelong   (d) merciless

_____(c)_____ 8. The jogger gave the policewoman his viewpoint of how the accident had happened and then <u>continued</u> jogging.

   (a) advised   (b) experienced   (c) resumed   (d) undertook

_____(c)_____ 9. There was such <u>a warmth of feeling</u> in the way the host greeted his guests that Jane was glad she had accepted the invitation to his party.

   (a) awareness   (b) politeness   (c) heartiness   (d) seriousness

_____(a)_____ 10. When the man in front of her at the check-out counter lit a cigar, Mrs. Stern tapped him lightly on the shoulder and <u>pointed to</u> the No Smoking sign hanging from the magazine rack.

   (a) indicated   (b) advertised   (c) promoted   (d) surveyed _____(d)_____ (11.) When the reporter asked the composer how he had created such a beautiful piece of music, he replied, "It was a wonderful idea followed by a lot of hard work."

(a) impression   (b) information   (c) innocence   (d) inspiration

_____(d)_____ 12. Whenever Peter ate in a restaurant, he was never very fussy about the food so long as the service was polite and prompt.

(a) particular   (b) impolite   (c) questioning   (d) regretful

後悔する

3 Compound Words.

3 **Compound Words.** To complete these sentences correctly, choose a word from List A and add a word from List B to it. If necessary, use a dictionary to help you complete this exercise.

List A	List B
after	brain
air	case
check	cob
cook	front
corn	line
fiddle(violin)	long
hay	mate
life	out
master	piece
mouth	post
scatter	sick
sea	stack
side	sticks
sign	swiped
stair	taste
water	wash

1. Driving his tractor up and down the field in a vain search for his

favorite ___corncob___ pipe which he had lost that morning,
トウモロコシの 穂軸

the farmer muttered, "This is like searching for a needle in a

___haystack___ ."

2. Karen was such a ___scatterbrain___ that she forgot she hadn't
そそっかしい人

taken her vacation trip to France yet and mindlessly threw away her

___airline___ ticket while cleaning out her purse.

3. "Oh ___fiddlesticks___ !" exclaimed a disappointed Aunt Polly
= Nonsense

when she heard the forecaster predict heavy thundershowers and

realized their ___cookout___ would have to be called off.
中止する.

4. Standing on the top step of the ___staircase___ Jimmy heard

his wife declare, "___Checkmate___ !" from the den below, and

was relieved that his wife had finally won the three-hour chess game,

that his brother-in-law would finally go home, and that they could go

to bed at last.

5. Stepping out the front door, Mr. Sutter's spirits sank to an all-time low when he discovered that some crazy fool had not only knocked over the ___signpost___ which advertised his carpentry business, but also had ___sideswiped___ his truck.

6. The four pieces of garlic bread Tim had eaten at the Madisons' housewarming party left an unpleasant ___aftertaste___ in his mouth that even gargling twice with ___mouthwash___ didn't help.

7. The workers on the ___waterfront___ stopped unloading the ship for a moment to watch the ___seasick___ passengers from the *S.S. Dreamboat* stagger down the gangplank.

8. While putting the last touches on the painting, the artist rejoiced that he had finally succeeded in his ___lifelong___ dream: to create a great ___masterpiece___.

4 **Review of Capitalization Rules.** Write five sentences which show that you have an understanding of at least *ten* of the fourteen rules you have studied. To help you recall the rules, they are listed below. Note that the example uses five of these rules.

Review of Capitalization Rules

1. Capitalize the first letter of the first word in a sentence.

2. Capitalize people's names.

3. Capitalize the word *I*.

4. Capitalize calendar items. Do not capitalize seasons.

5. Capitalize place names.

6. Capitalize the names of races, nationalities, and languages.

7. Capitalize special events.

8. Capitalize historical events and periods in history.

9. Capitalize names of business firms and brand names of business products.

10. Capitalize the names of organizations.

11. Capitalize the first word and all important words in titles of books, plays, movies, magazines, newspapers, stories, poems, works of art, and pieces of music.

12. Capitalize names referring to the one God of a religion, religions and their followers, and major religious writings. Do not capitalize the word *god* when it is used to refer to a religion with many gods.

13. Capitalize course names followed by a number and language courses. Do not capitalize the names of school subjects.

14. Capitalize East, West, North, and South when they refer to recognized sections of the country or of the world. Do not capitalize these words when they tell directions.

Example: When Mrs. Jackson left Joe's Meat Market, she couldn't remember whether she had parked her Ford on Hillside Avenue or Baker Street.

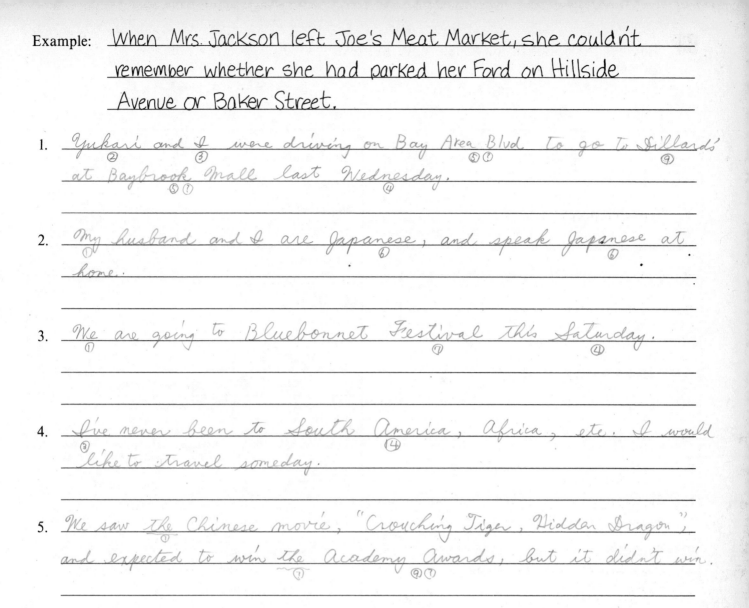

1. Yukari and I were driving on Bay Area Blvd. to go to Dillard's at Baybrook Mall last Wednesday.

2. My husband and I are Japanese, and speak Japanese at home.

3. We are going to Bluebonnet Festival this Saturday.

4. I've never been to South America, Africa, etc. I would like to travel someday.

5. We saw the Chinese movie, "Crouching Tiger, Hidden Dragon", and expected to win the Academy Awards, but it didn't win.

5

Looking for a Job. Use these classified advertisements to help you answer the questions which follow.

BABY SITTER NEEDED, in my own home. 3 children, hrs. 3pm—6pm. Mon-Fri. Refs a must. Own transp. 555-0213 between 10am-8pm.	DRIVER Earn extra cash after work or school. Need a warm, resp. person to pick up children after school & drive to lessons, etc. 3-4 days per week. Own car nec. Call 555-0117	RESTAURANT HELP WANTED: Kitchen help, bus people, waiters & waitresses, lunch & dinner shift. Please apply in person between 3-5pm, Mon-Fri, Cider Barrel Restaurant.	TIRE CHANGER, Experience preferred, but will train. Benefits, good salary. Call 555-4042 for appointment.
BARMAID, WAITRESS & PORTER. Full and part time. Starting week of 9-3. No phone calls please. Brookfield Bowling Center.	OFFICE CLERKS. Full time 9am-5pm & 4pm-11pm. High School Graduate with at least 6 months office experience. Newtown area. Call 555-2574, between 11am & 3pm	SALES HELP FOR CRAFT STORE, Part time 10am-5pm, 3 days per wk. Craft experience pref. but not necessary. Call 555-1776	TRUCK DRIVER, Must have class II Driver's license and be 21 years of age or older, 1st & 2nd shifts open. Call 555-2931 between 8am & 5pm.
BARTENDERS, WAITERS. Waitresses. Bus People. We are now hiring at Gregory's Restaurant. Experience necessary. Apply in person: 265 Federal Rd., Brookfield bet. 2-4.	PAINTER—If you have 5 yrs. experience as a painter and are making less than $9 an hr. Call after 5pm, 555-5622.	SALES PERSON — full time, Mon. thru Fri. 9am-5:30pm. Apply in person: English Drug. 140 South Ave.	TYPIST — Part time. 20 hrs. wk. Answer phones, general office duties. Call 555-2333
CHEF'S ASSISTANT experience preferred. Salary dependent upon experience. Immediate opening for hard working, creative individual Call 555-2567	PET SHOP CLERK Part Time 9am-1pm Call for appt. 555-3141	SALES—WEEKENDS PET SHOP. Must know birds and fish, more days avail. 555-2747.	WAITERS—WAITRESSES, Full and part time, all shifts available. Opportunity for advancement. Apply: Fiddler's Lodge
CHILD CARE—Before school care needed for 2 children. 3 mornings wkly. Excel. pay. Call 555-2011.	PHOTO STORE—Space Lab 1 Hour Foto now hiring. Full & part time positions available. Exper. helpful but will train. Call 555-3515	SERVICE AGENT POSITION—Part time for major car rental co. in Danbury. Responsibilities are servicing cars for rental. Weekends a must. Good pay and benefits. 555-5450 EOE m-f.	WAREHOUSE—Full time. We are in need of shipping, receiving and stock clerks, no exper. needed. Driver's lic. and a little knowledge of math needed. Call Mon-Fri. 9 am—4 pm, for application and interview, 555-8174.
CLEANERS-we have part time positions available, job inclds. wash. dry and folding of laundry. some counter work. Hrs. Sat. 8-4:30pm, or Wkdays 2pm-6pm. Call 555-7600 for more info.	PRESSER needed for shirt unit. Full time Tuesday-Saturday. $250-$350 per wk. depending on ability. Must be dependable. No experience necessary. Call Easy Cleaners, 555-1497	TELEPHONE SALES 25 hrs pr wk, day or evening hours Hourly plus commission. Phone 555-7355.	WOODWORKER WANTED, Hand & power tools, interesting work, good starting salary, will train right person. Call 555-1357, between 9 & 4, except Thurs.
CONTROL DESK PERSON am., pm. & weekends. No phone calls please. True Roll Bowling Lanes. 200 Federal Rd., Lancaster.		TELEPHONE SALES & APPOINTMENTS, 10 immediate positions. Part time mornings or evenings. No experience required. Call 555-0104. E.O.E.	

1. What do the following abbreviations stand for?

   (a) refs. _references_   (e) pref. _preffer_

   (b) transp. _Transportation_   (f) avail. _available_

   (c) wkly. _weekly_   (g) co. _cooperation_

   (d) resp. _responsible_   (h) lic. _licence_

2. Which two numbers would you call if you enjoy working with animals?

   Pet Shop Clerk and _Sales - Weekends_ Pet Shop

3. What does "hourly plus commission" mean in the TELEPHONE SALES ad?

   If you work more than 25 hours per week, you can get additional fee.

4. Name one ad you would respond to if you only wished to work part time.

   Baby Sitter.

5. Name one ad you would not respond to if you wanted to have your weekends free.

   Tire Changer.

6. What is E.O.E. an abbreviation for in the TELEPHONE SALES & APPOINTMENTS ad?

   _____

What do you think? Which job looks the best to you? What do you like about it?
Is there anything you don't like about it?

I would like baby sitter or waitress, because I like babies, kids, and like to talk to people. I don't want to do hard work, for example tire changer. I don't have much energy.

Find the Quote. Can you find this quote about work?

A. Each of the twelve descriptions defines or gives a clue for a certain word. Write that word on the lines to the left of each description.

B. Put the letters of these words in the blanks at the bottom of the page. The quote, when all the blanks are filled in, will be a thought about working.

C. The first one has been done for you. Study it before you begin.

P E N K N I F E
13 44 20 29 5 47 34 18

1. another name for a small pocketknife

N e w   Y e a r's   E v e
61 80 76 25 59 27 75 48   3 73 18

2. the holiday celebrated on December 31st (3 words)

p o s i t i v e
65 4 48 10 53 67 22 43

3. the antonym of negative

t e a k e t t l e
8 63 40 79 14 49 53 6 21

4. this whistles when the water is boiling

h o n o l u l u
2 45 70 72 39 60 28 60

5. the capital of Hawaii

t h i r t e e n
53 9 37 58 1 35 14 61

6. considered an unlucky number by many people

l i g h t h o u s e
6 19 12 54 1 50 15 60 48 35

7. a tall structure topped by a powerful light used as a signal to aid ships

t a d p o l e
52 69 81 16 30 38 23

8. an early stage of a frog or toad

D a d d y
68 57 62 71 56

9. Mommy's partner

a r t e r y   (動脈)
66 42 53 55 78 7

10. what carries blood away from the heart to all parts of the body

e n g i n e e r
74 11 41 33 46 80 14 24

11. the person who operates the train and waves to people from his cab

w a l l f l o w e r
36 51 6 32 31 17 77 26 44 64

12. a person, usually a woman, who doesn't enter into the fun at a social event because she is shy or unpopular

Quote: t h e   o N l y   t h i n g   P e o p l E   i N
            1 2 3   4 5 6 7   8 9 10 11 12   13 14 15 16 17 18   19 20

e v e r y   w a l K   o f   l i F e   w i l l   a g r e E
21 22 23 24 25   26 27 28 29   30 31   32 33 34 35   36 37 38 39   40 41 42 43 44

o n   I s   t h a t   t h e y   a r e   u n d e r p a i d
45 46   47 48   49 50 51 52   53 54 55 56   57 58 59   60 61 62 63 64 65 66 67 68

a n d   o v e r w o r k e d!
69 70 71   72 73 74 75 76 77 78 79 80 81

Unit 3
Going Places

An English author once wrote, "For my part, I travel not to go anywhere, but to go. I travel for travel's sake. The great affair is to move." Some people would not agree that traveling just for the sake of traveling is a good way to spend time. Most people, however, do enjoy being able to go places. In this unit, you will learn more about some people who have done—or tried to do—just that.

Mark Twain, the author of *The Adventures of Tom Sawyer*, is also the author of the reading for Lesson 11. Taken from his book *Life on the Mississippi*, this reading describes a tragedy which occurred when a Mississippi River steamboat blew up.

Someone once said, "More than anything else, the automobile expresses the American desire to be on the go." In the reading for Lesson 12, "The Automobile Revolution," a respected American writer explores the effects the automobile has had on our way of life.

As we learn in "Caught in Traffic," traffic jams can be caused by things other than cars. In this short story, the reading for Lesson 13, we see what happened to two people caught in a traffic jam.

The reading in Lesson 14, "A Ride in Space," deals with a very different kind of travel. Sally Ride, the subject of this reading, was the first American woman to travel in space.

You will encounter still another kind of travel in Lesson 15. Just as the title suggests, this selection describes a strange trip from "New York to France—in a Rowboat."

Lesson 11

Life on the Mississippi

Words for Study

Pennsylvania	tragic	conscious	modern
captain	ruins	patients	purchases
aboard	accommodated	wad	provided
pilothouse	adrift	chief	compliments
chimneys	moor	morphine	considerations
distances	naked	attendants	Jacuzzi

Life on the Mississippi

The reading selection below is taken from Mark Twain's book, *Life on the Mississippi*. In this selection, Twain describes a tragic steamboat accident that his brother was involved in. Twain, himself, was not on the boat. He was on another Mississippi steamboat and first learned of the accident when it pulled into a Mississippi town. But it was not until his boat reached Memphis, Tennessee, that he got the complete details. This is Twain's account of the accident.

* * *

It was six o'clock on a hot summer morning. The *Pennsylvania* was creeping along, north of Ship Island, about sixty miles below Memphis on a half-head of steam. The second mate had the watch on the deck. Most of the crew, including my brother Henry, were asleep. The captain was in the barber's chair, and the barber was preparing to shave him. There were a good many cabin passengers aboard, and three or four hundred deck passengers.

George was in the pilothouse—alone, I think—and he rang to "come ahead" full steam. The next moment four of the eight boilers exploded with a terrifying crash, and the whole forward third of the boat was hoisted toward the sky! The main part of the mass, with the chimneys, dropped upon the boat again. And then, after a little while, fire broke out.

Many people were flung great distances and fell in the river, including my brother. Some of the crew were never seen or heard of again after the explosion. The barber's chair, with the Captain in it and unhurt, was left with everything forward of it, floor and all, gone. The stunned barber, who was also unhurt, stood with one toe projecting over space, still stirring his shaving cream and saying not a word.

By this time, the fire was beginning to threaten. Shrieks and groans filled the air. A great many persons had been scalded, a great many crippled; the explosion had driven an iron crowbar through one man's body. Both mates were badly scalded, but they stood their posts, nevertheless. They drew a wood boat near, and the captain fought back the frantic herd of frightened passengers till the wounded could be brought there and placed in safety first.

When Henry and another crew member fell in the water, they struck out for shore, which was only a few hundred yards away; but Henry believed he was not hurt (what a tragic error!) and decided to swim back to the boat and help save the wounded. So they parted, and Henry returned.

By this time the fire was making fierce headway, and several persons who were imprisoned under the ruins were begging for help. All efforts to put out the fire proved fruitless. One of the prisoners said he was not injured, but he could not free himself. When he saw that the fire was likely to drive away the workers, he begged that someone would shoot him, and thus save him from the more dreadful death. The fire did drive the axmen away, and they had to listen, helpless, to this poor fellow's pleas till the flames ended his pain.

The fire drove all that could be accommodated into the wood boat the mates had pulled up; the boat was then cut adrift, and it and the burning steamer floated down the river toward Ship Island. They managed to moor the wooden vessel at the head of the island, and there, unsheltered from the blazing sun, the half-naked survivors had to remain for the rest of the day without food or help for their hurts. Finally, a steamer came along and carried them to Memphis. By this time Henry was no longer conscious. The physicians examined his injuries, saw he would not survive, and turned their main attention to patients who could be saved.

Forty of the wounded were placed upon straw-filled beds in a public hall, and among these was Henry. There, the ladies of Memphis came every day with flowers, fruits, and other gifts, and there they remained and nursed the wounded. All the physicians stood watches there, and all the medical students. The rest of the town furnished money or whatever else was wanted. Memphis knew how to do all these things well, for many a disaster like the *Pennsylvania's* had happened near her doors.

I watched there six days and nights, and a very sad experience it was. Two long rows of forms—and every face and head a shapeless wad of loose raw cotton. I saw many poor fellows removed to the "death room"—a room where the doomed were placed, so the others would not have to watch them actually die. The fated one was always carried out with as little stir as possible, and the stretcher was always hidden from sight. No matter: everybody knew exactly what was happening.

The chief mate was the only one who went to the death room and returned alive. His hurts were frightful, and he looked like nothing human. He was often out of his mind; and then his pains would make him carry on and shout and sometimes shriek. Now and then, he would tear off handfuls of the cotton and expose his cooked flesh to view. It was terrible.

The doctors tried to give him morphine to quiet him. But, in his mind or out of it, he would not take it. He said his wife had been killed by that drug, and he would die before he would take it. He was convinced that the doctors were concealing it in his medicine and in his water—so he ceased from putting either to his lips. Once, when he had been without water for two extremely hot days, he took the dipper, and the sight of the fluid and pain of his thirst tempted him almost beyond his strength; but he mastered himself and threw it away. After that he allowed no more water to be brought near him. Three times I saw him carried to the death room; but each time he revived, cursed his attendants, and demanded to be taken back. He lived to be mate of a steamboat again.

The main physician did all that sound judgment and trained skill could do for Henry; but, as the newspapers had said in the beginning, his hurts were past help. On the evening of the sixth day, his wandering mind busied itself with matters far away and his nerveless fingers picked at his blanket. His hour had struck; we bore him to the death room, poor boy.

Adapted from *Life on the Mississippi* by Mark Twain. Courtesy of New American Library.

1   **About the Reading.** If necessary, refer to the reading to answer the following questions correctly.

1. **Cause and Effect.** Match the effects with the causes listed below. Study the example before you begin.

Effects: ✓he begged the others to shoot him.
               ✓he returned to help rescue the wounded.
               he was able to work again as a mate on a steamboat.
               ✓Memphis knew how to respond to the accident.
               ✓the barber was stunned.
               ✓the captain was unhurt.
               ✓the chief mate refused both medicine and water.
               ✓patients for whom there was no hope were taken to the death room.
               ✓the physicians gave him less attention.
               ✓the wounded were taken to Memphis.

Causes:

1. Because the explosion was so sudden and terrifying, _the barber was stunned._

2. Because only a section of the barbershop blew up, _the captain was unhurt._

3. Because Henry believed he was unhurt, _he returned to help rescue the wounded._

4. Because one of the trapped persons aboard the steamer realized the fire would soon reach him, _he begged the others to shoot him._

5. Because another steamer came along, _the wounded were taken to Memphis._

6. Because of the seriousness of Henry's injuries, _the physicians gave him less attention._

7. Because steamboat disasters were not uncommon, _Memphis knew how to respond to the accident._

8. Because the physicians did not wish to frighten the patients, _patients for whom there was no hope were taken to the death room._

9. Because of the way his wife had died, _the chief mate refused both medicine and water._

10. Because the chief mate recovered from his injuries, _he was able to work again as a mate on a steamboat._

102   Lesson 11

2. What do you think? Mark Twain says very little about the death of his brother. Offer a reason that might explain his unwillingness to talk in detail about Henry's death.

He loved Henry very much, and was shocked by Henry's death. It was very tragic. Henry helped the wounded people and his injuries were terrible.

2 Synonyms and Antonyms.

Choose a synonym to fill in the first blank in each sentence. Choose an antonym to fill in the second blank. Study the example before you begin.

Synonyms		Antonyms	
abuse	✓naked	✓adrift	✓idle
✓active	✓offspring	✓ancestors	✓incorrect
compliment	✓precisely	✓clothed	insult
✓faultless	✓ruin	✓create	passing
✓formerly	seep	✓currently	tenderness
✓moored	✓unending	gush	✓vaguely

1. Secured and __moored__ are antonyms for __adrift__.

2. Bare and __naked__ are antonyms for __clothed__.

3. Mistreatment and __abuse__ are antonyms for __tenderness__.

4. Children and __offspring__ are antonyms for __ancestors__.

5. Destroy and __ruin__ are antonyms for __create__.

6. Praise and __compliment__ are antonyms for __insult__.

7. Lasting and __unending__ are antonyms for __passing__.

8. Exactly and __precisely__ are antonyms for __vaguely__.

9. Trickle and __seep__ are antonyms for __gush__.

10. Errorless and __faultless__ are antonyms for __incorrect__.

11. Previously and __formerly__ are antonyms for __currently__.

12. Busy and __active__ are antonyms for __idle__.

3 Idle Threats.

Idle Threats. Many threats are not idle, but the ones listed below provide a good way to review some common prefixes. Use the words listed at the left to complete each of these "idle" threats.

attend
contend 争う
extend
intend

1. *What the wealthy aunt said to her selfish niece:*

   "I don't care what you ___intend___ to do this evening! I
   ___contend___ that if you don't ___attend___ yourself and
   ___extend___ my wedding like any dutiful niece would, I shall cut you out
   of my will faster than you can say 'three million dollars'!"

interview
overview (概観)
preview
review

2. *What the governor said to his newest staff member:*

   "Just to give you a ___overview___ of what we're in for—if we don't
   ___review___ our monthly reports and try to form some kind of an
   ___preview___ of our progress to date, we're going to look like a bunch of
   fools at the press ___interview___!"

advise
devise (工夫する)
revise (修正する)
supervise

3. *What the plant manager said to the foreman:*

   "If you can't ___devise___ a better system when you ___revise___
   this stupid plan tonight, I shall ___advise___ the company to find someone
   else to ___supervise___ this important project!"

admit (～を許す)
commit (～を犯す)
submit (～を提出させる)
transmit (～を送る)

4. *What the captain of the security guard said to the traitor:*

   "If you don't ___admit___ that you were about to ___commit___ an
   act of treason in attempting to ___transmit___ a message to the enemy, I
   shall ___submit___ a request to have your entire family brought in for
   questioning."

they should conserve the energy not waste

conserve (～を保存する)
deserve (～を受ける価値がある)
preserve (～を保持する)
たもつ保護する
reserve

5. *What the young lady said to her boyfriend:*

   "If you don't ___reserve___ good seats for the concert, you might as well
   ___conserve___ gas and not even come over here that evening because you
   don't ___deserve___ any more of my time, and nothing will
   ___preserve___ this relationship!"

compose (〜を書く) 6. *What the coach said to the soccer player:*
dispose
expose
impose (〜を負わせ)

"I hate to ___*impose*___ on you just before the game, but if you don't

___*dispose*___ of the garbage in your locker immediately, I shall

___*compose*___ a note for the bulletin board and ___*expose*___ every

one of your sloppy habits to the entire team!"

compress (押しつける) 7. *What the wife said to her husband, who was running for the city treasurer's seat in*
depress
express
impress

the November election:

"You say writing these speeches and talking to crowds ___*impress* / *depress*___ you;

but I say if you don't ___*depress* / *compress*___ your ideas about tax reform into much

shorter statements and learn to ___*express*___ yourself in a more interesting

way, you're going to ___*compress* / *impress*___ the voters as nothing but a long-winded

bore!"

contract (契約する) 8. *What the dentist said to a patient:*
detract (〜を損とす)
extract (〜を抜く ≥ pull out)
subtract (〜を引く)

"If you refuse me permission to ___*extract*___ this rotten tooth, not only

will you ___*contract*___ even more serious dental problems, but also your

diseased mouth will ___*detract*___ from your overall appearance and

___*subtract*___ years from your life!"

---

4 **Contractions.** A contraction is a shortened word formed by leaving out or combining some of the letters. Write the contractions for the following words. Study the examples before you begin.

1. is not	isn't		7. it is	It's
2. I am	I'm		8. I would	I'd
3. do not	don't		9. I shall	I'll
4. does not	doesn't		10. he will	he'll
5. did not	didn't		11. you are	you're
6. she is	she's		12. you have	you've

5 **Traveling by Steamboat.** Mississippi steamboat trips are still a popular form of adventure for many Americans. If you haven't been discouraged by the Mark Twain reading and if you have a few thousand dollars to spare, you might want to plan a steamboat trip on the Mississippi some day. For your information, some facts about modern-day steamboat travel have been listed below. Use this information to answer the questions which follow.

IMPORTANT STEAMBOAT INFORMATION
(listed in alphabetical order)

Air Conditioning: All vessels are fully air-conditioned.

Baggage: Baggage is not limited as long as it is in keeping with the length of the cruise. Properly mark your name and cabin number on your baggage tag. A porter will meet you at the gangway to take your baggage to your cabin.

Clothing: Men usually wear a coat and a tie to dinner. Women wear a dress, a "dressy" skirt, or a pantsuit.

Cruise Fares: Fares include transportation, cabin, meals, and on-board entertainment. Fares do not include personal items such as wine, photographs, gift shop purchases, or laundry.

Deck Chairs and Towels: These are provided compliments of the steamboat company.

Handicapped: The handicapped are welcome aboard the ship. Doorways accommodate a standard size wheelchair. However, bathroom doorways will not accommodate wheelchairs. The steamboat company requests anyone requiring a wheelchair to have a traveling attendant to assist him/her.

Health Considerations: Doctors are not part of the boat's staff because of the nearness to shore and the many shore stops.

Insurance: It is suggested for your self-interest that you have insurance to cover anything that might occur during your trip. This service is available through insurance agents and most travel agents.

Jacuzzi: Located on the sun deck, the Jacuzzi is open year-round and heated to suit the temperature of the day.

Passage Contract: Passengers are to carefully review their passage ticket before boarding. This contract describes our legal relationship with you and you will be asked to sign it upon boarding.

Personal Funds: Payment for onboard charges may be made by cash, personal check, travelers checks or the American Express Card.

Pets: Pets of any kind are not permitted on board.

Third Persons: Third persons may share the cabin of two other full-fare passengers at the rate of $75.00 per night.

---

1. What do they call the rooms in which the passengers sleep on a steamboat?

    Cabin.

2. Why would you probably pack your best clothes if you were to go on this trip?

    Because I need nice dress to have dinner.

3. While on a steamboat, what would you do if you suddenly needed a doctor?

    I'll ask a staff to stop the steamboat and go to see a doctor.

4. Whom do you contact to make sure you have the necessary insurance?

    I contact my insurance agent.

5. Why would a person in a wheelchair need an attendant traveling with him or her?

    Because bathroom doorways don't accommodate wheelchairs.

6. How much would you have to pay if you wanted to rent a deck chair?

    It's free.

7. On which deck is the Jacuzzi located? _It's on the sun deck._

8. Name an item you might purchase which is not included in your fare.

    Wine, beer, soft drinks, souvenir.

9. Why does the steamboat company advise you to read your ticket?

    Because the contract is described and I need to sign it upon boarding.

10. Do you think you would enjoy the steamboat company's cruise? Be sure to support your answer.

    Yes. I've never travel on steamboat and I think I can enjoy it. I can sleep on a boat every night, and can visit many places when a boat stops. I also can enjoy dinner at the dinning room, and relax in a jacuzzi every day.

Lesson 12

The Automobile Revolution

Words for Study

revolution	windshields	privacy	criminals
snobbishness	minimum	source	introduced
average	motorcycle	conflict	mph
garages	popularity	junior	absorbers
carriage	introduction	envy	sober
motorists	expensive	reckless	yield

The Automobile Revolution

In 1906, a president of an American university stated that the automobile offered a picture of the snobbishness of wealth. Yet just less than twenty years later, an American housewife, in response to a comment on the fact that her family owned a car but no bathtub, uttered a fitting theme song for the automobile revolution: "Why, you can't go to town in a bathtub!"

When the automobile ceased to be a symbol of wealth for the few and became a need for the many, great changes in American life occurred. These changes, however, did not occur overnight. They could not. For they depended on three things. First, a car had to be made that the average American could afford, depend upon, and take care of without too much difficulty. Second, good roads had to be built. And third, garages and filling stations had to be plentiful. All these three requirements came slowly. A man who had tried to operate a filling station beside a dusty country road in 1906 would have speedily gone broke. It wasn't until the 1920s that the impact of the automobile revolution was felt most sharply from year to year.

When the university president spoke in 1906, and for years afterward, the automobile was a noisy thing that couldn't seem to make up its mind whether it was a machine or a horse-drawn carriage. Whenever you went for a drive—if you were wealthy enough to afford a car—you never knew just what to expect. Each car had a toolbox on the running board and motorists were used to carrying with them blowout patches, French chalk, and tire irons against the awful moment when a tire would pop miles from any help. The motorist had to crank the engine by hand—a difficult and sometimes dangerous business. Most cars were open, with windshields which gave only a minimum of protection against wind and dust to those in the back seat. Goggles were widely worn. Going for a ride in one of the early cars was much like riding on a motorcycle.

Then there was the problem of the roads. Roads were mostly dusty or muddy with no through routes. Even as late as 1921, there was no such thing as a numbered highway. In that year the *Automobile Blue Book* advised motorists to have a shovel with them for

Adaptation of "The Automobile Revolution" from *The Big Change: America Transforms Itself 1900-1950* by Frederick Lewis Allen. Copyright 1952 by Frederick Lewis Allen. Reprinted by permission of Harper & Row, Publishers, Inc.

mountain roads, sandy stretches, and muddy places. In the early days of the automobile, horses were a danger for the driver, and speed limits set by country towns were sometimes low indeed. One American recalls that in a farming town in New Hampshire, the first legal limit was six miles an hour.

When Henry Ford was able to drive down the price of the automobile, automobiles became more popular. Equally responsible for the automobile's increasing popularity was a series of important improvements such as the invention of a self-starter in 1912. Perhaps the most important improvement was the introduction of the closed car. As late as 1916, only 2 per cent of the cars made in the United States were closed; by 1926, 72 per cent of them were. What had happened was that the automobile makers had learned to build closed cars that were not extremely expensive, did not rattle themselves to pieces, and could be painted with a fast-drying, lasting paint.

Meanwhile, the car-buying public discovered with delight that a closed car was something quite different from the old "horseless carriage." It was a power-driven, storm-proof room on wheels that could be locked and parked all day and all night in all weathers. You could use it to fetch home the groceries, cool off on hot evenings, reach a job many miles away, or visit distant friends. Young couples were quick to learn the privacy that this room on wheels gave them. Also, of course, the car often became a source of family conflict: "No, Junior, you are *not* taking the car tonight!"

Some people argued that the automobile destroyed the healthy habit of walking, weakened the churchgoing habit, promoted envy, killed innocent people when driven by reckless and drunken motorists, and provided criminals with a safe getaway. Nevertheless, the automobile was here to stay.

So it was that the years between 1918 and 1930 introduced to America a long series of new features which are now such a common part of the American scene that it is easy to imagine that they've always been around: traffic lights, concrete roads with banked curves, six-lane highways, motels, used-car lots, and roadside diners.

No such change in the habits of a nation could have taken place without having far-reaching social effects. Let us glance at a few of them:

1. The number of Americans whose home and place of employment were at least twenty miles apart vastly increased. As more and more people whose living was dependent upon work in the city fled to the outskirts for homes, city planners became concerned about the future of the city.

2. The automobile expanded Americans' sense of geography. One could still find, here and there, men and women who had never traveled farther from home than the county seat, but their number was shrinking fast.

3. The automobile revolution brought sudden death. As cars became more powerful and roads became straighter and smoother, the number of people slaughtered yearly by cars in the United States increased. The shocking death toll led to more cautious licensing of drivers, the inspection of cars, an increased number of warning signs along the roadsides, and studies of the causes and cures of death on the highway.

4. The automobile age brought a parking problem that was forever being solved and then unsolving itself again. The question, "Where do I park?" is as annoying today as it has been at any time since the beginning of the automobile revolution.

5. The automobile revolution gave birth to a new kind of personal pride. The American might feel shame because he is poor, has an unimportant job, or by any other circumstance that might make him feel unworthy in his own eyes. But when he slides behind the wheel of an automobile, and it leaps forward at his command, this "unworthy soul" can imagine that he is truly "king of the road."

1 **About the Reading.** Put the letter of the correct answer in the blank to the left.

_____ 1. The period which marked the greatest impact of the automobile on American life was _____ .

    (a) 1900–1910   (b) 1905–1915   (c) 1910–1920   (d) 1920–1930

_____ 2. Henry Ford helped to make the automobile more popular when he _____ .

    (a) applied paint that would last to his cars
    (b) constructed closed cars
    (c) invented the self-starter
    (d) made cars that people could afford

_____ 3. Based on the university president's statement in 1906, we can conclude that he _____ .

    (a) had little idea that the automobile would create such far-reaching changes in American life
    (b) believed poor people shouldn't own automobiles
    (c) had never had the pleasure of riding in an automobile
    (d) was filled with envy because he couldn't afford a car

_____ 4. The early motorists wore goggles so they _____ .

    (a) could see the bumps and ruts in the road better
    (b) would have some protection
    (c) would look stylish
    (d) would not be recognized by their friends

_____ 5. The group that seemed to be against the automobile in the early days was _____ .

    (a) criminals   (b) housewives   (c) farmers   (d) young lovers

_____ 6. One reason cited by the author to explain the death toll on the highways is _____ .

    (a) the improvement of road conditions
    (b) the lack of warning signs
    (c) the number of people who worked in the city but no longer lived there
    (d) the widespread use of cars by criminals

_____ 7. A driver who feels as if he is "king of the road" experiences _____ .

    (a) pride   (b) greed   (c) envy   (d) royalty

_____ 8. Because of the Automobile Revolution, the number of _____ decreased.

    (a) criminals   (b) diners   (c) homebodies   (d) housewives

(c)   9. The author refers to the introduction of the automobile as the "Automobile Revolution" because _____ .

(a) people gave up things they needed in order to buy a car
(b) poor people could now consider themselves as important as wealthy people
(c) so many changes occurred in the way Americans lived
(d) the American cities began to fall apart

(d)   10. The author's main reason for writing this passage seems to be _____ .

(a) to argue the need for the American public to know more about the automobile
(b) to describe the viewpoints of those who thought the automobile was a terrible invention
(c) to explain the dangers introduced by the automobile
(d) to present the early history of the automobile

2 **What Do You Think?** In the early 1900s, few people imagined that the automobile would become a popular form of transportation. Using your imagination, describe what you think will be the most popular form of travel for people living one hundred years from now.

We can't travel far away by car. Because there are many car troubles, and there are not many filling stations beside roads. Roads are not adjusted, there are bumps, and I don't want to drive for a long time.

3 · Word Relationships. For each of the following statements, choose the best answer and write it on the line.

1. Earache is to painful as ____ (a) ____ .
   (a) disaster is to tragic (c) revolution is to modern
   (b) purchase is to expensive (d) survivor is to unhurt

2. Plentiful is to scarce as ____ (d) ____ .
   (a) harsh is to serious (c) merciful is to forgetful
   (b) long-winded is to talkative (d) taut is to slack

3. Razor is to barbershop as ____ (c) ____ .
   (a) attendant is to hospital (c) drill is to dentist's office
   (b) dentist's office is to drill (d) hospital is to attendant

4. Abbreviate is to shorten as ____ (a) ____ .
   (a) alter is to revise (c) dismiss is to hire
   (b) clutch is to yield (d) hassle is to supervise

5. Automobile is to motor as ____ (d) ____ .
   (a) bicycle is to handlebar (c) jet is to pilot
   (b) carriage is to wheels (d) train is to engine

6. New Hampshire is to New England as ____ (c) ____ .
   (a) Michigan is to the East (c) Oklahoma is to the West
   (b) North Carolina is to the South (d) Pennsylvania is to the Midwest

7. Expensive is to cheap as ____ (d) ____ .
   (a) devise is to provide (c) positive is to imagined
   (b) extract is to remove (d) sober is to silly

8. "Fiddlesticks!" is to expression as ____ (b) ____ .
   (a) letters are to alphabetical order (c) she will is to contraction
   (b) mph is to abbreviation (d) rules are to capitalization

9. Conserve is to waste as ____ (a) ____ .
   (a) bloom is to wilt (c) submit is to reflect
   (b) redden is to blush (d) subtract is to multiply

10. Lifeboat is to steamer as ____ (d) ____ .
    (a) engineer is to train (c) passenger is to taxi
    (b) brakes are to bicycle (d) parachute is to airplane

4 **The Prefix *un*-.** The most common prefix is *un*- which means *not*. Use the words at the left to complete each sentence correctly.

undesirable
unexpected
unfastened
unfruitful
ungrateful (感謝を表さない)
uninformed
uninterested
unleashed (解放する)
unlimited
unsafe
unskilled
untrue

1. It is simply _____untrue_____ that the automobile has had very little impact on how we live.

2. Blacksmiths found the popularity of the automobile particularly _____undesirable_____ because, in a few short years, they found themselves out of work.

3. Tommy was completely _____uninterested_____ in the fact that his sister needed a way to get home from play practice. All he knew was that it was *his* night to use the family car.

4. One reason that Americans are so _____uninformed_____ about the nation's transportation problems is that most newspapers confine their reporting of transportation issues to strikes and tragic accidents.

5. As Joe _____unsafe / unfastened_____ his safety belt, he delicately rubbed his aching stomach and wondered if the extra money he was earning as a driving instructor was worth an ulcer.

6. Most attempts to improve the transportation system in the United States have been _____unfruitful_____ because neither the city, state, nor federal governments have had a clear idea of what the goals should be.

7. Mrs. Wade was stunned when her husband presented her with a brand-new car for her fiftieth birthday; the gift was totally _____unexpected_____ .

8. Of the 142 million tons of gases, soot, chemicals, and acids which are _____unleashed_____ into the skies of the United States each year, 82 million tons come from automobile, truck, and bus exhausts.

9. "A bunch of _____unskilled_____ boneheads must have worked on my car at that garage!" roared Mr. Valentine as his Volkswagen spluttered to a grinding halt in the middle of nowhere.

10. In the best-selling book, _____unfastened / unsafe_____ at Any Speed, the description of how dangerous automobiles were finally prompted the federal government into forcing the automobile industry to make safer cars.

11. "You know, if you weren't so _____ungrateful_____ , people who give you lifts might be more willing to take you exactly where you want to go," the truck driver remarked after studying the look of resentment on the hitchhiker's face.

12. If everyone could drive at _____unlimited_____ speed, what do you think highway travel would be like?

5   **More Work with Contractions.** Write the contractions for the following words.

1. we would   _we'd_

2. they would   _they'd_

3. she will   _she'll_

4. he will   _he'll_

5. we are   _we're_

6. they have   _they've_

7. he is   _he's_

8. how is   _how's_

9. there is   _there's_

10. has not   _hasn't_

11. were not   _weren't_

12. madam   _ma'am_

6 **Taking a Written Driver's Test.** Here are some sample questions from the Connecticut driver's test. Circle the letter of the answer you think is correct. Then see how well you scored by comparing your responses with the answers which appear at the end of the test.

1. What is the minimum following distance you should leave when driving behind a motorcycle?

   (a) 2 seconds   (b) 4 seconds   (c) 6 seconds

2. At 50 mph, the distance required to stop a car is about:

   (a) 1/4 block   (b) 1/2 block   (c) 3/4 block

3. Which of the following can cause problems when you're not moving?

   (a) bad brakes   (b) bad shock absorbers   (c) bad exhaust system

4. You are driving in city traffic. How far ahead should you be looking?

   (a) about 25 feet   (b) about 1 block ahead   (c) about 2 blocks ahead

5. To cross a stream of traffic in the city from a full stop, you need a gap of:

   (a) 100 feet   (b) 1/2 block   (c) a full block

6. If you have had too much to drink, you can sober up by:

   (a) drinking hot coffee
   (b) taking a cold shower
   (c) waiting several hours

7. When driving on a road covered with packed snow, you should reduce your speed by:

   (a) 1/2   (b) 1/3   (c) 3/4

8. A traffic light with a flashing red signal means:

   (a) Caution   (b) Yield   (c) Stop

9. If the rear of your car begins to skid sideways, you should:

   (a) pump the brakes
   (b) apply the brakes gently
   (c) stay off the brake

10. If you are driving car 1, in which of the following pictures (A, B, or C) would it be most difficult to see car 2?

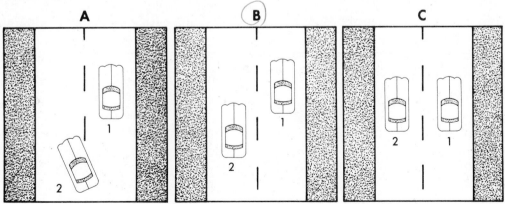

Answers: 1. b 2. b 3. c 4. b 5. b 6. c 7. a 8. c 9. c 10. b

Lesson 13

Caught in Traffic

Words for Study

Anthony	gallop	Manhattan	mythology
servant	nephew	angel	myth
generations	furniture	devil	Apollo
encyclopedia	reins	rascal	weapons
society	vehicles	Cupid	apostrophe
Broadway	impatiently	pierces	contradicts

Caught in Traffic

Old Anthony Rockwall, who had made millions in the soap business and was now retired, looked out the library window of his Fifth Avenue mansion and grinned. "Mike!" he shouted to his servant in the voice he had used in his younger days on the Great Plains. "Tell my son to come in here before he leaves the house."

When young Rockwall entered the library, the old man looked at him with kindly seriousness. "You're a gentleman," said Anthony finally. "They say it takes three generations to make one, but they're wrong. Money will do it as slick as soap grease. It's made you one. By golly! It's almost made one of me."

"There are some things that money can't buy," remarked young Rockwall gloomily.

"Now, don't say that," said old Anthony, shocked. "I bet my money on money every time. I've been through the encyclopedia down to Y looking for something you can't buy with it."

"For one thing," answered Richard, "it won't buy one into the best circles of society."

"Ah," said Anthony keenly. "What's her name?"

Richard began to walk up and down the library floor.

"Why, she'll jump at you!" exclaimed Anthony. "You've got the money and the looks, and you're a decent boy. Your hands are clean. You've got no soap on 'em. You've been to college, but she'll overlook that."

"I'm too late. She's going to sail for Europe. I'm allowed to meet her with a cab tomorrow evening at Grand Central Station. We drive down Broadway at a gallop to Greenwood Theater, where her mother will be waiting for us in the lobby. Do you think she would listen to me tell her how much she means to me during those six or eight minutes under those circumstances? No, Dad, this is one tangle that your money can't unknot."

"All right, Richard, my boy," said old Anthony cheerfully. "You may run along now."

At eight o'clock the next evening, Richard's aunt took an old ring from a moth-eaten case and gave it to Richard. "Wear it tonight, nephew," she begged. "Your mother gave it to me. Good luck in love she said it brought. She asked me to give it to you when you had found the one you loved."

Young Richard took the ring and tried it on his smallest finger. It slipped as far as the second joint and stopped. He took it off and stuffed it into his vest pocket. And then he phoned for his cab.

At 8:32 that evening, Richard met his true love at Grand Central Station. "We mustn't keep Mother waiting," said she.

"To Greenwood Theater as fast as you can drive!" said Richard loyally.

The carriage whirled up Forty-second to Broadway. Then at Thirty-fourth Street, young Richard quickly thrust up the trap and ordered the driver to stop. "I've dropped a ring," he explained, as he climbed out. "It was my mother's, and I'd hate to lose it. I won't keep you a minute—I saw where it fell."

In less than a minute he was back in the cab with the ring.

But within that minute a cross-town car had stopped directly in front of the cab. The cabman tried to pass to the left, but a heavy express wagon cut him off. He tried the right, but had to back away from a furniture van that had no business being there. He tried to back out, but dropped his reins and swore dutifully. He was stuck in a tangled mess of horses and vehicles.

"Why don't we drive on?" said Richard's true love impatiently.

Richard stood up in the cab and looked around. He saw a flood of wagons, trucks, cabs, and vans filling the vast space where Broadway, Sixth Avenue, and Thirty-fourth Street cross one another. The entire traffic of Manhattan seemed to have jammed itself around them.

"I'm very sorry," said Richard as he resumed his seat, "but it looks as if we are stuck. They won't get this mess cleared for about an hour. It was my fault. If I hadn't dropped the ring we—"

"Let me see the ring," said the young lady. "Now that it can't be helped, I don't care. I think theaters are stupid anyway."

At eleven o'clock that night somebody tapped lightly on Anthony Rockwall's door.

"Come in," shouted Anthony, who was in a red dressing gown, reading a book about pirates.

Somebody was Richard's aunt, looking like a gray-haired angel that had been left on earth by mistake. "They're engaged, Anthony," she said softly. "She has promised to marry our Richard. On their way to the theater there was a traffic jam, and it was two hours before their cab could get out of it. And oh, Brother Anthony, don't ever boast of the power of money again. A little symbol of true love—a little ring—was the cause of our Richard's finding his happiness. What good could your money have done?"

"Sister," said Anthony Rockwall. "I've got my pirate into a devil of a scrape. His ship has just sunk, and he's too good a judge of the value of money to let it drown. I wish you would let me finish this chapter."

The story should end here. I wish it would (as heartily as you who read it) wish it did. But we must go to the bottom of the well for truth.

The next day a person with red hands and a blue necktie, who called himself Kelly, called at Anthony Rockwall's mansion and was at once received in the library.

"Well," said Anthony, "let's see—you had $5,000 in cash."

"I paid out $300 more of my own," said Kelly. "I had to go a little above our figure. I got the express wagons and cabs mostly for $5; but the trucks and two-horse teams mostly raised me to $10. The motormen wanted $10, and some of the loaded teams $20. The cops stuck me hardest—$50. But didn't it work beautiful, Mr. Rockwall?"

"Thirteen hundred—there you are, Kelly," said Anthony, tearing off a check. "Your thousand, and the $300 you were out. By the way," Anthony said to Kelly who was about to leave, "you didn't notice anywhere in the tie-up a kind of a fat boy without any clothes on shooting arrows around with a bow, did you?"

"Why, no," said Kelly, puzzled. "I didn't. If he was like you say, maybe the cops nabbed him before I got there."

"I thought the little rascal wouldn't be on hand," chuckled Anthony. "Good-bye, Kelly."

Adapted from "Mammon and the Archer" by O. Henry with permission of Airmont Publishing Company, Inc. New York, New York.

1   **About the Story.** Write the letter of the correct answer on the line to the left.

_(d)_   1. The setting of the story is _____ .

     (a) Chicago   (c) Los Angeles
     (b) Detroit   (d) New York

_(a)_   2. For which of the following does Anthony Rockwall seem to lack respect?

     (a) formal education   (c) Richard
     (b) reading   (d) money

_(X)(c)_   3. When Anthony Rockwall tells his son his "hands are clean," he means _____ .

     (a) Richard bathes regularly
     (b) Richard is not a criminal
     (c) Richard is not a worker but a gentleman
     (d) Richard has never been in love before

_(b)_   4. Richard's true love begins to relax after _____ .

     (a) Richard has asked her to marry him
     (b) Richard has told her they are in a bad traffic jam
     (c) Richard has met her at Grand Central Station
     (d) the cross-town car has blocked their cab

_(b)(c)_   5. Anthony Rockwall _____ his sister's claim that it was the ring that has brought Richard and his true love together.

     (a) agrees with   (c) ignores
     (b) disagrees with   (d) scorns

_(d)_   6. From the aunt's statements, we can guess that Richard's mother _____ .

     (a) died from a broken heart
     (b) had died when Richard was a baby
     (c) was responsible for her husband's success
     (d) was quite different from her husband

_(a)_   7. Whom did Kelly have the most trouble bribing?

     (a) the police   (c) the cabmen
     (b) the motormen   (d) the truck drivers

_(b)_   8. Who regrets that the story doesn't end before the scene in which Kelly pays a visit to the Rockwall mansion?

     (a) Anthony Rockwall   (c) Kelly
     (b) the author   (d) the cabmen

_(c)_   9. Although the story doesn't reveal the name of the "fat boy without any clothes on," who do you think he is?

     (a) Apollo   (c) Cupid
     (b) Bacchus   (d) Pan

_(b)(a)_   10. If you had no idea what the answer to the last question was, you had company. Which character in the story has no idea who the "fat boy" is?

     (a) Kelly   (c) Richard's aunt
     (b) Richard   (d) Richard's love

2 More Prefixes That Mean *Not*.

In addition to *un-*, five other prefixes can mean *not*: *il-*, *im-*, *in-*, *ir-*, and *non-*. Use the words at the left to complete the sentences correctly. Use each word only once.

illegal ⓐ (非合法の)
impatient
improper (不適当な)
impure
indecent ⓑ (下品な)
independent
indigestion ⓑ (不消化)
indirect ⓐ (遠回しの)
inexperience
insane ⓐ (正気でない)
irresponsible ⓐ (責任を負わない)
nonmetal (非金属)
nonsense
nonskid ⓐ (滑らない)

1. When you drink __impure__ water, you may be in grave danger.

2. If you suffer from __indigestion__ ~~impatient~~, you may be headed for an ulcer.

3. The selling of whiskey to minors is __illegal__.

4. An __irresponsible__ ~~independent~~ person cannot be depended upon.

5. Because of their __inexperience__, many new employees are given training programs by their employers.

6. Oxygen is an example of a __nonmetal__.

7. An __independent__ ~~irresponsible~~ state or country is one that is self-governing.

8. A person who speaks in an __indirect__ way has trouble making himself understood.

9. The word __nonskid__ might be on your mind if you were shopping for a new set of tires.

10. __Improper__ describes the clothing of a person who attends a formal wedding dressed in blue jeans, a sweat shirt, and sneakers.

11. __Indecent__ describes how a person would be regarded if he or she showed up at a formal wedding stark naked.

12. The actions of a madman can be described as __insane__ ~~nonsense~~.

13. You might reply, "__Nonsense__ ~~Insane~~!" when somebody tells you a story that you regard as silly or untrue.

14. If you have completed this exercise in an __impatient__ ~~indigestion~~ manner, you may have made quite a few errors.

3 A Fat Boy without Any Clothes On.

The "fat boy" to whom Anthony Rockwall referred in the story is Cupid. Use the words listed below to complete this passage about the Roman god of love.

arrows   deadly   pierced   sorry
bowstring   escape   plea   sprinted
create   eyes   prayed   supposed
crown   perched   reject   wildness

Cupid

In Roman mythology, Cupid is the god of love. He is often pictured as a chubby baby or child with wings who carries a bow and _____arrows_____ . With these arrows, he gaily _____pierced_____ the hearts of men and women.

Sometimes Cupid is shown blindfolded to stress the _____wildness_____ of his shooting. Also, some of his arrows were _____supposed_____ to be tipped with gold to _____create_____ strong love in his victims' hearts. The rest of his arrows—which had lead tips—caused his victims to _____reject_____ the love shown by others.

In one myth, Apollo, the Roman god of the sun, came upon Cupid, who was stringing his little bow. Apollo told him to leave the _____deadly_____ weapons to grownups and play with toys instead.

Smirking, Cupid continued to string his bow. When he was finished, he _____perched_____ on a ledge and took two arrows—one gold and one lead.

He put the lead arrow in his _____bowstring_____ and hit the heart of a lovely young maid. A moment later, he shot Apollo with the arrow of love just as Apollo's _____eyes_____ fell upon the lovely young maid.

Certain that she would return his love, Apollo _____sprinted_____ after her. But the young maid tried to _____escape_____ . When she realized that he was about to catch her, she _____prayed_____ to her father, a river god, to save her. Her father answered her _____plea_____ , and as Apollo reached her, she suddenly changed into a tree. Confused, he asked, "Why don't you like me?"

As the wind blew through the leaves, they answered, "I don't know." Then the tree felt _____sorry_____ for Apollo and gave him a gift—a _____crown_____ of leaves that would never die. Apollo put the crown on his head and sadly went on his way. Cupid had won again!

4 **The Apostrophe to Show Ownership.** The punctuation mark you used to write contractions in Lessons 11 and 12 is called an *apostrophe*. An apostrophe is also used to show ownership. Below are two examples using the apostrophe to show ownership. Study them carefully. Then rewrite the remaining phrases in the same way.

1. the impression of Polly — *Polly's impression*

2. the uniform of the cheerleader — *the cheerleader's uniform*

3. the costume of the actress — *the actress's costume*

4. the effects of the morphine — *the morphine's effect*

5. the coffeecake of Mrs. Mack — *Mrs. Mack's coffeecake*

6. the masterpiece of the screenwriter — *the screenwriter's masterpiece*

7. the wings of the angel — *the angel's wings*

8. the hives of the beekeeper — *the beekeeper's hives*

9. the discovery of the chief — *the chief's discovery*

10. the tantrums of Jackie — *Jackie's tantrums*

11. the atmosphere of the earth — *the earth's atmosphere*

12. the patients of the psychiatrist — *the psychiatrist's patients*

5 **Money.** Throughout the ages, much has been written about money. Put a check before the sayings cited below that might just as easily have been said by Anthony Rockwall.

_√_ A fool and his money are soon parted.

_____ A lack of money is the root of all evil.

_√_ How pleasant it is to have money!

_____ If a man is wise, he gets rich, and if he gets rich, he gets foolish, or his wife does. That's what keeps the money moving around.

_____ If making money is a slow process, losing it is quickly done.

_√_ Make money, money by fair means if you can; if not, by any means.

_√_ Money alone sets all the world in motion.

_____ Prefer to store money in the stomachs of the needy rather than hide it in a purse.
give it to the poor   keep it yourself
_____ Put not your trust in money, but put your money in trust.
Don't trust money   put your money safe place
_√_ Remember that time is money.

_√_ There are three faithful friends—an old wife, an old dog, and ready money.

_√_ Though mothers and fathers give us life, it is money alone which preserves it.

Now choose any one of the sayings above and describe an experience you've had which either supports or contradicts the saying.

When I was a student, I didn't have a lot of money. When I got the first paycheck, I was very happy, because I felt I became independent. I bought presents for my family. Then I could buy anything I wanted travel anywhere, eat anything. It was worth it for me to earn my living.

6 **More about Money.** When old Anthony Rockwall finished his pirate book, he might have enjoyed reading a poem like "The Rich Man" by Franklin P. Adams (1881–1960). After you've read the poem, answer the questions which follow.

The Rich Man
by Franklin P. Adams

The rich man has his motor-car,
　His country and his town estate.
He smokes a fifty-cent cigar
　And jeers at Fate.
He frivols through the livelong day,
　He knows not Poverty her pinch.
His lot seems light, his heart seems gay,
　He has a cinch.
Yet though my lamp burns low and dim,
　Though I must slave for livelihood—
Think you that I would change with him?
　You bet I would!

1. What do you think *frivols* means in the first line of the second verse?

   It means that living idle without work, spending lots of
   It means care free (Don't care of important things.) money.

2. Explain what *lot* means as it is used in the third line of the second verse.

   (It means fate.) or Its role.

3. Does the poet seem to agree or disagree with old Anthony Rockwall's belief about money? Support your answer with evidence from the poem.

   It seems to disagree. Because this poem expresses negatively
   against the rich man, for example "He frivols".
   He agrees. He wants to be rich. Because "You bet I would !".

4. Do you agree with the poet, or do you hold a different belief about money? Be sure to explain your thoughts in detail.

   Yes. Because I don't like to being idle, spending lots
   of money. My ideal life is "work hard then enjoy
   a lot."

Lesson 14

A Ride in Space

Words for Study

astronaut	capsule	radiator	remote
NASA	Soviet Union	assumed	retrieve
amnesia	attracted	resourceful	announced
shuttle	cosmonaut	assigned	satellite
launch	apron	designing	stow
orbiting	opinions	manipulator	cartoonist

A Ride in Space

In 1977, when Sally Ride was 25 years old and finishing up her studies at a California university, she spotted a notice in the school newspaper about openings in the astronaut program, a career that she had never even considered previously. She was up and out of the room before she had finished reading the notice, one of more than 1,000 women and nearly 7,000 men to apply for what would be the 35 slots in the astronaut class of 1978.

How NASA chose 35 people from the 8,000 applicants remains a mystery, although Ride's husband claims to have found one important key. When asked by the NASA psychiatrist whether they had ever had amnesia, all the successful applicants seemed to have answered, "I don't know, I can't remember." Sally Ride must have given this response also, for she and five other women were among those accepted into NASA's class of 1978.

Six years later, on June 18, 1983, she and four other astronauts, all men, strapped themselves into seats on the flight deck of the space shuttle Challenger and, 44 minutes and 23.7 seconds after its thunderous launch, reached the final orbiting position beyond the fringe of the earth's atmosphere. This six-day mission was the seventh in the shuttle series and the second for the Challenger.

Thus, 22 years, 36 manned missions, and 57 astronauts after the first space capsule splashed into the Atlantic Ocean, Sally Ride became the first woman to wear the Stars and Stripes in space. Space itself is not expected to be changed much by the event, but it was surely an important moment for women. Ride herself stated to a reporter, "I did not come to NASA to make history. It's important to me that people don't think I was picked for the flight because I am a woman." Yet this was in fact one of the things NASA had in mind when Ride and the other women were accepted into the astronaut program. As a woman employee at the Johnson Space Center delicately explained, "At that time in our country, people were feeling a little bit bad about the way they had treated women."

Women had been in space before, although they had hardly left their mark on it. The first time was almost exactly 20 years before Sally Ride's flight aboard the Challenger. The woman was a 26-year-old factory worker and sky diver from Russia. She was launched aboard a rocket shortly before the Soviet Union was to serve as host to the World Congress of Women. The event attracted much public attention, although reports since then have held that the woman was sick for most of the three-day mission. Then, in August, 1982, in plenty of time to beat Ride's timetable, the Soviets launched their second woman cosmonaut, a 34-year-old test pilot and parachute ace. When her spacecraft docked with the orbiting Soviet space station, one of the two male cosmonauts manning the space station joked that he had an apron ready for her.

Like the Russians, Americans did not ignore the fact that Sally Ride is a woman. American newspaper and television reporters hounded Ride for her thoughts and opinions about being the first American woman in space and often complained that they were having trouble getting much information from her. Reporters demanded to know if Ride planned to wear a bra. "There is no sag in zero G," she explained. Reporters wanted to know if she cried when she had a problem. "Why doesn't someone ask the pilot of the shuttle mission those questions?" she responded with a smile. The pilot, of course, was a man.

Ride's answers to reporters were in keeping with her sister Karen's description of her: "Sally lives up to her own standards. What other people think of her is not of the highest importance to her. She doesn't run around trying to make everyone happy, which most women tend to do."

In trying to describe some of the qualities that may have been responsible for Ride's success, Molly Tyson, her college roommate, recalled the time Sally's car broke down on a dark and deserted road, laid low by a burst radiator hose. Tyson assumed there was nothing to do but curl up in the back seat and wait for help to happen by. Ride, however, quickly created a repair with a roll of Scotch tape buried in the trunk, found a saucepan rattling around in back, and set off down the road in search of water. Within an hour they were back on the road. "I imagine she's going to be very resourceful up there in space," Tyson commented.

It was also one of the few times Tyson saw Ride pick up a saucepan. A government agent interviewed Tyson as part of a background check on Ride. "I only lied once," she recalled, "but I figured that dust and dirty dishes wouldn't collect in a space capsule the way they had in our apartment."

Tyson has also offered information about the Ride family, which she described as not at all your normal family: "They didn't have to sit at the same table for dinner. People ate dinner when they wanted, and they could have a whole dinner of nuts and cheese and crackers." In one sense, that was an ideal home for bringing up an astronaut; for Sally considers space food on the whole as "pretty good."

In Ride's first years with NASA, she was assigned to work on the team designing a manipulator arm for the shuttle, an engineering job that bore little relationship to her university training. Operated by remote control, the manipulator arm would send out and retrieve experiments. "I spent two years on it, and nothing else," Ride recalled. "As far as I knew, there was nothing else; what you did was launch an arm."

No one was surprised when the director of flight operations announced that Ride would be a member of STS-7, the second Challenger mission. The manipulator arm was first used on this mission. One of Ride's tasks during this space flight was to use the arm to snatch a 3,960-pound shuttle satellite floating in space and stow it in the cargo bay.

In addition to being the first American woman in space, Ride's life is unusual in that she is married to another astronaut. Ride has said that she doesn't plan to have children, which seems to have more to do with her feelings about raising children than it does with her career. Her father remembered that the first time Sally had a babysitting job, the children refused to eat the sandwiches she had made because she put the peanut butter and jelly in the wrong order. She threw the sandwiches out, made another batch, and never took another babysitting job again.

1 **About the Reading.** Put the letter of the best answer on the line to the left.

_(b)_   1. What was most unusual about Ride's prompt response to the notice about openings in the astronaut program in her school newspaper?

(a) Her college background had not prepared her to become an astronaut.
(b) She had never even considered becoming an astronaut.
(c) She was applying for a man's job.
(d) She was twenty-five years old and hadn't yet finished school.

_(a)_   2. NASA's reason for accepting Sally Ride and her classmates in the astronaut program was ____ .

(a) all of them had a good sense of humor
(b) none of them had ever suffered from amnesia
(c) they were the best applicants
(d) unknown

_(d)_   3. Sally Ride was a member of the second Challenger mission which was launched into space in ____ .

(a) 1977   (b) 1978   (c) 1980   (d) 1983

_(c)_   4. Sally Ride was the ____ .

(a) only woman in space   (c) first American woman in space
(b) first woman in space   (d) second woman in space

_(a)_   5. Who thought that Sally Ride's launch into space was an important event for women?

(a) the author of the article   (c) Ride's husband
(b) Sally Ride   (d) Ride's father

_(d)_   6. When Ride stated "As far as I knew, there was nothing else; what you did was launch an arm," she probably meant ____ .

(a) she had no desire to be part of the Challenger mission
(b) she was totally involved in her work on that project
(c) she was disappointed that she had been assigned to that project
(d) she thought that was all there was to the space program

_(a)_   7. Sally Ride doesn't plan to have children because ____ .

(a) she doesn't want any   (c) her husband doesn't want any
(b) she is too busy with her career   (d) she is getting too old

_(c)_   8. Who seemed most willing to be interviewed by reporters?

(a) Ride's father   (c) Ride's college roommate
(b) Ride's husband   (d) Ride's sister

_(d)_   9. Based on this reading, which word _least_ describes Sally Ride?

(a) adventurous   (b) private   (c) resourceful   (d) tidy

2 **Understanding Cartoons.** Study the cartoon below and then answer the questions that follow.

© 1983 Jim Borgman—Cincinnati Enquirer
Reprinted with the permission of King Features Syndicate, Inc.

1. What do the reporters seem to be most interested in?

   They seem to know the difference between a female astronaut and male one.

2. Which feature of the reporters' faces do you most notice? Why do you think the cartoonist has enlarged this feature?

   The reporter who said that I told you women were too emotional for this kind of work.

3. What is Ride's reaction to the press? How do you know?

   She doesn't want to answer. Because she goes by.

4. Whose side does the cartoonist seem to be on in this cartoon? Be sure to offer a reason for your answer.

   Ride's side. She doesn't answer questions at all because she thinks those questions are nonsense.

5. Does the cartoonist's picture of the press agree with the description given in the reading passage? Be sure to offer evidence for your answer.

_____

_____

6. Does the cartoonist's picture of Sally Ride agree with the description given in the reading passage? Again, be sure to cite evidence to support your answer.

_____

_____

_____

_____

_____

3 **Facts and Opinions.** A *fact* is a statement that can be proven to be true or false. An *opinion* is a personal thought or attitude about something. Write *fact* beside each of the following statements that is a fact. Write *opinion* if the statement is an opinion.

opinion   1. Most women tend to run around trying to make everyone happy.

fact   2. Sally Ride's sister once commented that most women tend to run around trying to make everyone happy.

fact   3. Reporters asked Sally Ride many personal questions.

opinion   4. Reporters should ask anyone in the news as many personal questions as they can so the American public can be informed.

opinion   5. The president of the United States should only be allowed to serve one four-year term of office.

fact   6. In the U.S., presidential elections are held every four years.

opinion   7. A woman's place is in the home.

fact   8. In 1920, women were granted the right to vote.

opinion   9. Television is a wonderful way to bring the family closer together.

opinion   10. The average American watches too much television.

4 **The Prefix re-.** The prefix *re-* has two common meanings: *again* (for example, rerun) and *back* (for example, replace). Choose the word from each set which completes the sentence correctly and write it in the blank.

renew
reopen
retrieve

1. The lawyer was certain that the judge would _____ the case since new evidence had recently come into his possession.

reforming
rerunning
retracing

2. Annabel had spent most of the afternoon ___*retracing*___ the steps of her hectic morning, but her efforts were in vain. She still couldn't find her purse.

recycling
reorganization
reunion

3. His high school class's twenty-fifth ___*reunion*___ was coming soon, but Mr. Beech was having second thoughts about attending, because he had gained quite a few pounds and lost quite a few hairs.

reconstruction
recount
replacement

4. The loser often demands a ___*recount*___ after a close election if he either suspects foul play or clings to the hope that he might be the winner after all.

recounted
rephrased
retraced 引き返す

5. William ___*rephrased*___ his answer after noting the puzzled expression on the interviewer's face and hoped that his confusing response hadn't ruined his chances of getting the job.

refit 修理する
refuel
repossess 取り戻す

6. When Pat learned that the bank was about to ___*repossess*___ her brother-in-law's car, she finally agreed to lend him the money, even though she knew she'd probably never see it again.

reconsider
reconstruct
refit

7. Joe's doctor was able to successfully ___*reconstruct*___ his shattered leg bone after his terrible automobile accident. 物語する

redouble
regain
retrace 再考する

8. "Don't worry. If we ___*regain*___ our efforts, things will work out just fine," the foreman cheerfully advised, in an effort to raise the workers' sagging spirits after they had just experienced a setback. 敗北

rebuild
reclaim
replant

9. As part of his evidence to ___*replant*___ 15,000 acres for the tribe, the lawyer presented a treaty signed by the federal government in 1837 which proved that the land had been granted to the Indians.

reversing
revising 作り直す
revoking 無効にする

10. The court slowed Lucy to a walk by ___*revoking*___ her license after she had received three traffic tickets in one month.

5 **More Work with the Apostrophe.** Use the example to guide you as you rewrite the following phrases.

1. the apron of the butcher   *the butcher's apron*

2. the skyline of Manhattan   *Manhattan's skyline*

3. the cousins of Tony   *Tony's cousins*

4. the radiator of the Volkswagen   *the Volkswagen's radiator*

5. the fractured arm of Jack   *Jack's fractured arm*

6. the cage of the gerbil   *the gerbil's cage*

7. the journey of Francis   *Francis' journey*

8. the servants of Mr. Royal   *Mr. Royal's servants*

9. the orbit of the satellite   *the satellite's orbit*

10. the lounge of the clinic   *the clinic's lounge*

11. the routine of the veterinarian   *the veterinarian's routine*

12. the halo of the angel   *the angel's halo*

6 **Compound Words.** To complete these sentences correctly, choose a word from List A and add a word from List B to it. If necessary, use a dictionary to help you complete this exercise.

List A	List B
candle	boat
dare	breakers
guess	bush
handy	coming
heavy	cord
home	devil
look	joyed
motor	light
over	man
rip	out
road	robe
rose	stone
tight	wad
tomb	weight
ward	work
Wind	work

1. Betsy was such a ___daredevil___ that the airplane pilot prayed she wouldn't wait until the last possible second to pull the ___ripcord___ of her parachute.

2. Her cousin had always loved gardening so much that, after her funeral, Dr. Duke planted a ___rosebush___ in front of her ___tombstone___ .

3. Mr. Kennedy was such a ___tightwad___ that he was always on the ___lookout___ for inexpensive little items at yard sales that he could use as Christmas and birthday gifts.

4. The boys were glad they had brought their ___windbreakers___ to protect them from the cool breeze when they took their ___motorboat___ out for a spin on the lake.

5. The trainer warned the _____ boxing champ that if he didn't stop clowning around and start taking his ___heavyweight___ more seriously, he might as well kiss his title good-bye.

6. Wendy went through every item of clothing in her ___wardrobe___ and then burst into tears because she didn't have a single thing to wear to the ___homecoming___ dance after the football game.

7. When James was unable to repair the kitchen ceiling light, his wife gently reminded him that he had never been much of a _____—to which he spitefully replied, "At least if we eat by ___candlelight___, I won't have to look at the leftovers you're always serving me."

8. Were you ___handy___ that you immediately knew the answers to this exercise, or were your answers mostly the result of ___guesswork___ ?

Lesson 15

New York to France—in a Rowboat

Words for Study

Samuelson	anchor	Norwegians	giant
Brooklyn	kerosene	routine	instant
fortune	biscuit	glorious	emergency
voyage	discarded	canvas	supply
compass	liquor	megaphone	Amazon
sextant	gathered	progress	Caribbean

New York to France—in a Rowboat

Strange as it may sound, two men once rowed across the Atlantic Ocean in an open boat—the full 3,250 miles from New York to France. Yet today the Atlantic adventure and the names of its heroes are forgotten.

Frank Samuelson and George Harbo, two men from Norway, lived in Brooklyn and dredged for oysters off New Jersey. In 1896, the year of their daring adventure, Harbo was 30 and Samuelson 26, but both had spent their lives at sea and possessed a strength far greater than their average builds suggested.

"If anybody would row the ocean," Samuelson had told Harbo, "he would make a fortune. People would pay to see the boat." One man couldn't do it, they had agreed, but two men might make the voyage in two months, if they rowed 54 miles a day. So why not try it?

Harbo, a licensed boat pilot, figured out that the best route was eastward by way of the Gulf Stream and the North Atlantic drifts. These currents would add slightly to the speed of a craft going in their direction. Further, this was the heavily traveled North Atlantic shipping route, which promised help in the event of disaster.

For two years, the Norwegians devoted their spare time to completing plans. Finally, they designed a double-pointed, 18-foot craft, with a five-foot beam and eight-inch draft. At both ends were watertight compartments and tanks for drinking water. Into the boat went five pairs of oars, a compass, a sextant, a sea-anchor, an air mattress, signal lights, and five gallons of kerosene for the small stove rigged in the bow. Richard K. Fox, a newspaper publisher, paid for the construction of the boat, and the little white oak craft was named *Fox* in his honor.

Their food included 250 eggs, 100 pounds of sea biscuit, nine pounds of coffee, and plenty of canned meat. All clothing except oilskins and what they were wearing was discarded. No tobacco, liquor, or sails were taken aboard.

A crowd of 2,000 gathered the afternoon of June 6, 1896, to see them off. The weather was perfect, but there was an air of gloom. "This is suicide," was a common comment.

"We'll see you all in France or in heaven!" shouted Harbo cheerfully as the *Fox* pushed off. Harbor whistles saluted the boat as it skimmed down the bay with both Harbo and Samuelson rowing. When the *Fox* passed out to sea, the two Norwegians began their routine, which called for 15½ hours of rowing a day for each man. At first, the weather was glorious; but trouble began with the oil stove. It was hard to keep lighted even in a mild breeze. They had little coffee and soon had to eat their eggs raw.

On the fourth night out, Harbo was asleep under the canvas shelter. Suddenly, he sat up and cried: "Something bumped us!"

As they listened, it came again, a bump and a scrape across the bottom. Then, something white flashed in the dark water alongside.

"A shark!" said Harbo.

For two days the shark swam with the boat while the oarsmen, undisturbed, continued their rowing.

A week out, the adventurers met a schooner bound from Canada to New York.

"Come alongside and we'll take you aboard!" the captain shouted through his megaphone.

"No thanks," Samuelson shouted back. "We're on a voyage."

"Where are you bound?"

"Europe."

With her crew shaking their heads, the Canadian ship sailed on.

The next day, Sunday, the oarsmen experienced their first bad weather. A heavy gale blew up from the east, almost dead ahead. Waves rose higher and higher until they washed over the *Fox*. At 9 A.M. the two men gave up rowing and tossed out the sea anchor. By 5 P.M., Harbo figured that their progress for the day had been 25 miles backward!

Ten days later, a German ship came into sight. Harbo hoisted an American flag, and the steamer responded with her colors.

"Are you shipwrecked?" the steamer's skipper shouted.

"No. Bound for Europe."

"Are you crazy?"

"No, indeed." On the Norwegians rowed, sometimes singing, but usually pulling their oars in silence.

On July 7 a westerly gale blew up, and for two days the exhausted oarsmen battled huge waves. It was a grim fight. Ten times a day the tiny craft had to be bailed out. Then, on the second night, a giant wave bore down on them.

"Look out!" shouted Samuelson.

"We'll never clear it!" gasped Harbo.

In an instant the *Fox* was overturned and the two men were struggling in icy water. But even for this emergency they had made plans. Each wore a life belt, fastened to the boat by rope.

Also, the keel had been provided with a rail to which the voyagers could cling.

After several attempts, they righted the boat, crawled aboard and began desperately to bail. Some of their food had been swept away; their clothes were soaked. Sleepless and hungry, they presented a sorry sight as the sun rose over a quieter sea. They stripped and wrung out their soaked clothing. Then they resumed rowing to take the stiffness from their swollen joints.

But there were other problems. Wind, sun, and salt water had turned the backs of their hands into raw flesh. An even graver problem was their low food supply. While previously it had been amusing to joke with passing vessels, it was now a matter of life or death to hail one.

Help appeared on July 15 in the shape of a vessel bound for Canada. The oarsmen tied a blanket to an oar and began to wave it. At last, the ship turned toward the starving oarsmen. The vessel turned out to be from their birthplace in Norway. After a joyful reunion with seamen like themselves, the two adventurers filled the *Fox's* water tanks, stocked her with fresh food, and continued their voyage.

With half their voyage behind them, the weather continued fair and for more than a week they averaged 65 miles a day. On August 1 they sighted land—the southwestern tip of England. On August 7 their voyage ended when Samuelson and Harbo stepped ashore in France to the cheers of thousands.

Did the men make the fortune they had dreamed of? No. The problem was that the rowboat that had crossed the Atlantic looked just like any other rowboat, and people would not pay to see it. Greatly disappointed, both men disappeared from the public spotlight and finally went back to Norway. In 1946, Samuelson died in an old people's home. The Norwegian newspapers were kinder to him in death than they had been in life. "The world will not soon see his like again," wrote one reporter.

Adapted from "New York to France—in a Rowboat" by Tom Mahoney. Copyright © 1948 by Esquire Associates.

1 **About the Reading.** State whether the following quotes from the reading passage are statements of fact or statements of opinion. Then explain the reason for your answer in good sentence form. Be sure to use information from the reading to support your answer.

1. "We'll see you all in France or in heaven!"

_____

_____

2. "Something bumped us!"

_____

_____

3. "We'll never clear it."

_____

_____

4. "This is suicide."

_____

_____

5. "If anybody would row the ocean, he would make a fortune."

_____

_____

6. "The world will not soon see his like again."

_____

_____

2 **What Do You Think?** Describe a situation in which you might be willing to risk your life for a fortune. Remember that fortune does not always refer to money. Fortune can refer to success in general.

_____

_____

_____

_____

3 **Synonyms.** Match each word listed at the right with its synonym.

agreement
bulletin
conflict
consideration
decrease
faraway
furthermore
glorious
illegal
nerveless
occupation
suspect

_____

_____

_____

_____

_____

_____

_____

_____

_____

_____

_____

1. announcement

2. banned

3. distrust

4. livelihood

5. moreover

6. pact

7. reduce

8. remote

9. splendid

10. struggle

11. thoughtfulness

12. unafraid

4 **Antonyms.** Match each word listed at the right with its antonym.

abbreviate
ashore
defense
disperse
heavenly
inexperienced
irresponsible
manmade
reckless
remote
retrieve
watertight

_____

_____

_____

_____

_____

_____

_____

_____

_____

_____

1. aboard

2. cautious

3. dependable

4. discard

5. gather

6. leaky

7. lengthen

8. natural

9. nearby

10. offense

11. veteran

12. worldly

5 **The Prefix *pre-*.** The prefix *pre-* means *before* or *happening earlier in time*. Use the words listed at the left to complete the following sentences correctly.

precooked
predated
preheat
prehistory
prejudged
premedical
prepay
preschool
preshrunk
pretest
preview
prewar

1. "I'm sorry I was so harsh with you. I guess I _____ you as a lousy actress, but your work tonight proved I was dead wrong," the producer said sheepishly after Jill's faultless performance on opening night.

2. Anthony hoped that, although he had forgotten to _____ the oven, it wouldn't affect the new recipe he was preparing for his guests that evening.

3. At 3:30 the _____ children left the zoo and were pleasantly surprised when the adults treated them to ice cream sodas before dropping them off at their homes.

4. Franklin thought that if he _____ the rent check, his landlord might believe that the only reason his payment was late was that he had forgotten to mail it.

5. "If this movie is anything like the _____," remarked Pearl, "it's going to win the prize for most boring picture of the year."

6. Months before the first shot was fired, the _____ movement of troops made the people of Europe tense and uneasy.

7. On the first day, the students took a _____ so the instructor would have a fairly good idea of how much they already knew about auto repair.

8. Until reading that her new pantsuit had been _____, Miss Hooker was uncertain about whether she could wash it.

9. Figuring out how to earn enough money for _____ school was the next step, once Herb decided he wanted to be a psychiatrist.

10. _____ is the study of mankind in the period before written or recorded history.

11. Simply having to heat up the _____ ham made preparing dinner take only a few minutes.

12. Learning that he had to _____ for the tools he wanted to send for, Mr. Cooper replied, "Forget it. I don't fork over my hard-earned money for anything until I see it."

6 **Bodies of Water.** Use a dictionary, encyclopedia, atlas, or almanac to answer the following questions. To save yourself some time and effort, skim all the questions before you begin.

1. Match each word at the left with its definition.

lake   _____   A. a large body of salt water that is completely or partly
ocean   surrounded by land or is a tract of water within an ocean
river

sea   _____   B. a large inland body of fresh or salt water

        _____   C. a large natural stream of water emptying into an ocean, lake, or other body of water

        _____   D. the entire body of salt water that covers about 72 per cent of the earth's surface

2. Place the bodies of water listed below in their proper categories. Use each name only once.

Amazon   Dead   Louise   North
Arctic   Great Salt   Michigan   Pacific
Atlantic   Huron   Mississippi   Snake
Caribbean   Indian   Nile   South China

Lakes	Oceans	Rivers	Seas

3. Use the bodies of water in Question 2 to answer these questions.

a. What is the world's longest river? _____

b. What is the earth's largest body of water? _____

c. Which sea is located north of South America? _____

d. Which lake is located in the state of Utah? _____

e. Which lake is located entirely in the country of Canada? _____

1   **Word Review.** Use the words listed below to fill in the blanks correctly.

Amazon	megaphone	poverty
Broadway	morphine	reins
capsule	myth	satellite
compass	Nile	sextant
generation	oilskin	shuttle

_____   1.   a compartment of an aircraft or spacecraft designed to accommodate a crew; a covering for a dose of medicine

_____   2.   a compound extracted from opium; repeated doses cause addiction

_____   3.   a device used to figure geographical direction; also, a V-shaped device used for drawing circles

_____   4.   a funnel-shaped device used to direct and make one's voice louder

_____   5.   a river in eastern Africa

_____   6.   a river of South America which flows north and then east to the Atlantic Ocean

_____   7.   a small body orbiting a planet

_____   8.   a story dealing with gods, goddesses, ancestors, and heroes

_____   9.   a train, bus, or plane making short trips between two points; a device used in weaving to carry a thread back and forth between other threads

_____   10.   an instrument used by seamen to measure the height of heavenly bodies

_____   11.   cloth treated with oil so that it is waterproof

_____   12.   long, narrow leather straps used by a rider or driver to control a horse or other animal

_____   13.   the average length of time between the birth of parents and the birth of their offspring

_____   14.   the main theater district of New York City

_____   15.   the state or condition of being poor

2 **Word Review.** Write the letter of the best answer on the line to the left.

_____ 1. A patient who has amnesia suffers from _____ .
 (a) acid indigestion   (c) high blood pressure
 (b) eyestrain   (d) memory loss

_____ 2. What is the capital of the Soviet Union?
 (a) London   (b) Moscow   (c) Paris   (d) Warsaw

_____ 3. Which word describes a person who is able to make the most out of what is available?
 (a) accommodating   (b) fearless   (c) independent   (d) resourceful

_____ 4. If you wanted to learn more about the god Apollo, in which section of the library would you look?
 (a) geography   (b) history   (c) mythology   (d) travel

_____ 5. Which word describes your chances of winning the lottery?
 (a) endless   (b) plentiful   (c) remote   (d) unlimited

_____ 6. Which word describes your likely reaction if you learned you had indeed just won the lottery?
 (a) irresponsible   (b) stunned   (c) sober   (d) ungrateful

_____ 7. For which of the following do you have to knead dough?
 (a) cupcakes   (b) doughnuts   (c) corn bread   (d) pancakes

_____ 8. A snobbish person usually lacks _____ .
 (a) compassion   (b) opinions   (c) envy   (d) self-interest

_____ 9. Which country would you visit if you wanted to see the Nile River?
 (a) Egypt   (b) Japan   (c) Norway   (d) Russia

_____ 10. Which word means to store away in a neat and compact way?
 (a) reconstruct   (b) refit   (c) stint   (d) stow

_____ 11. Which government agency is _not_ concerned with investigating criminal activities?
 (a) CIA   (b) FBI   (c) IRS   (d) NASA

_____ 12. A synonym for _behold_ is _____ .
 (a) gaze   (b) glance   (c) glare   (d) grasp

_____ 13. If you assume something is true, you _____ .
 (a) doubt that it is true
 (b) have confirmed that it is true
 (c) hope that it is true
 (d) take for granted that it is true

_____ 14. Which of the following is often considered a symbol of good fortune?

(a) a cat's paw   (c) a peacock's feather
(b) a coonskin cap   (d) a rabbit's foot

_____ 15. Which symbol is often used in a cartoon when one of the characters has an inspiration?

(a) a giant   (c) a question mark
(b) a light bulb   (d) an anchor

3 **How Would You Classify It?** Match the words in the list at the left with their proper categories. Use each word only once.

astronaut	_____	1. NASA employee
barrel		
Challenger	_____	2. color
cinnamon	_____	3. container
cosmonaut		
Cupid	_____	4. firearm
encyclopedia		
kerosene	_____	5. fuel
moon	_____	6. god
motorcycle		
rifle	_____	7. instrument
scarlet		
sextant	_____	8. mammal
whale	_____	9. reference book
	_____	10. Russian space program employee
	_____	11. satellite
	_____	12. spacecraft
	_____	13. spice
	_____	14. vehicle

4 **Facts and Opinions.** Write four examples of statements of fact and four examples
of statements of opinion. Study the examples before you begin.

Facts

Example: In 1867, the United States purchased Alaska
            for $7.2 million.

1. _____

2. _____

3. _____

4. _____

Opinions

Example: The least pleasant season of the year in the
            Northeast is winter.

1. _____

2. _____

3. _____

4. _____

5   **Review of the Apostrophe and Capitalization.** In the sentences below, 29 words need to be capitalized. Also, three words in each sentence need apostrophes. Rewrite each sentence below, making the necessary changes.

1. ever since shed read the story of cupid in her brothers greek mythology book, kate wished that such a god really did exist who would shoot an arrow of passion into dr. springtimes heart.

_____

_____

_____

_____

2. "id meet you at grand central station, but manhattans traffic is so bad youd be better off just taking a taxi to west end avenue," adam told aunt mary, who was coming to visit for the weekend.

_____

_____

_____

_____

3. "theyll never have time to visit grants tomb if theyre planning to spend the afternoon in central park," said tom who quickly added, "but then, who wants to see a tomb on such a glorious autumn afternoon."

_____

_____

_____

_____

4. after reading the article about sally rides life in an old issue of *time* magazine at the dentists office, tony was certain that her work on the challenger had been much more relaxing than all the interviews shed had to suffer through.

_____

_____

_____

_____

6 Five-Letter Words.

- The letters of the word in each box can be used to form another word. Use the clues to help you figure out what that other word is.
- Then put the number of the clue into the circle. The circled numbers in each row and column will add up to 34.
- After you have figured out a word, write its first letter in the correct blank at the bottom of the page. When all the blanks are filled in, you will have spelled the name of the world's largest inland sea.
- To help you, the first and last clues have been filled in.

MOORS ⑦ ROOMS	TUNAS ⑨ AUNTS	AMONG ① MANGO	DREAD ⑯ ADDER	= 34
BELOW ② ELBOW	FLIER ⑦ RIFLE	LEASE ⑮ EASEL	KNEAD ⑩ NAKED	= 34
HEART ⑪ EARTH	KNITS ⑭ STINK	RELAY ⑥ EARLY	LIVED ③ DEVIL	= 34
THORN ⑬ NORTH	ASIDE ④ IDEAS	RANGE ⑫ ANGER	BLEAT ⑤ TABLE	= 34

= 34   = 34   = 34   = 34

Clues

1. A fruit that rhymes with tango
2. the joint between the forearm and upper arm
3. In paintings and cartoons, he is often pictured with horns, a tail, and carrying a pitchfork.
4. Thoughts or opinions
5. Like people, this piece of furniture has legs
6. An antonym for late
7. A firearm designed to be fired from the shoulder
8. Kitchens and dens are examples of ____ .
9. The sisters of your mother and father
10. Nude or unclothed
11. The third planet from the sun
12. A feeling of rage
13. The opposite of south
14. To give off a strong, foul smell
15. A stand for an artist to put his canvases on
16. A kind of snake

The world's largest inland sea:

M E D I T E R R A N E A N   S E A
1 2 3 4 5 6 7 8 9 10 11 12 13   14 15 16

Unit 4
Food

Food is the theme of this last unit in Book 6. The reading for Lesson 16, "As American As Apple Pie," describes the importance of the apple in colonial America and tells how Johnny Appleseed came to be a famous American folk hero.

"Save Your Stomach," the reading for Lesson 17, presents information about what our bodies do with the food we eat. As the title suggests, it also encourages us to give serious thought to our eating habits.

What is mealtime like for an American family? The reading for Lesson 18 shows how one family acts as its members gather for their morning meal. This reading, "A Breakfast Scene," is taken from a famous play entitled *A Raisin in the Sun*.

In "Taste Treats," the reading for Lesson 19, the author describes some of the practices of the people whose job it is to get food from the farm to the supermarket shelves.

Finally, in Lesson 20, "The Wizard of Alabama" describes the life of George Washington Carver—an American scientist whose experiments with plants did much to improve both the diet and general quality of many people's lives.

Lesson 16

As American As Apple Pie

Words for Study

especially	transformed	foreign	frontier
orchards	vinegar	native	endure
colonies	methods	adapted	warrior
colonists	puddings	insecticides	sear
plague	variety	affairs	villages
material	agriculture	Indiana	portrayed

As American As Apple Pie

Apples have always been important in America, especially in the North. In fact, planting apple orchards was among the first tasks the settlers in the early colonies undertook. Crab apple trees were already growing wild in the woods of North America when the settlers arrived, but they made no effort to put these trees in orchards. Instead, like Johnny Appleseed, they grew their trees from seeds. Only they used seeds imported from Europe.

Apples were important for many reasons. Very high on the list was as a source of cider. The colonists needed something to drink, but they did not consider the pure drinking water in America because they were in the habit of avoiding the water in Europe—for good reason. For the most part, water in Europe was so impure that it wasn't worth one's life to drink it. In England, for example, it was the standard practice when someone died of plague for his survivors to throw his bedding into the nearest lake or river. So the only choices the American colonists considered as reasonable drinks were ones they were used to—beer and wine of some sort or another. Hard cider is actually classified as a wine.

In addition to drinking cider, the colonists used it as the raw material for other important products. For one thing, cider was easily transformed into cider vinegar. The vinegar was used in pickling, one of the important methods of preserving vegetables and fruits for winter before the coming of canned goods.

Apple cider also could be used to make a type of brandy popularly called applejack. When strong enough, the applejack could be used to preserve fruits such as peaches, plums, and cherries. Beyond that, strong spirits, including apple spirits, found plenty of use in early medicine.

Beyond cider and its by-products, apples were used as food for livestock which were allowed to graze in early orchards and, of course, as food for the colonists themselves. The expression "as American as apple pie" wasn't the product of a poet's imagination. Apple dishes of one kind or another could be found at just about every colonist's meal, especially in New England. The apple was made into pies and fritters and puddings—a host of dishes.

One quality that made apples especially popular in the early American kitchen was that they lasted. If handled gently and stored with care in October, they might keep until the following March. Apples that would not keep in storage could be dried or made into apple butter.

Often apples for drying were peeled, and the peels and cores were dried separately for later use in brewing a kind of beer.

In colonial America, apples were popular not just because of their wide variety of uses. The apple trees did not require a lot of attention. Insects apparently did not attack the trees or the apples to the extent they do today. When reading old records of American agriculture, one seldom finds references to insect damage. The plants and fruits that the colonists introduced to this country were foreign to the diets of the native insects. As long as their native foods were available in the forests, these insects stayed pretty much in the wilderness.

But when the forests were replaced by farms, native insects adapted themselves to the new conditions. In addition, insect pests from Europe were introduced into America, concealed among the plants and seeds that the colonists and later generations brought with them. It sometimes took years for the foreign insects to adapt fully, but they did.

Insecticides were introduced during the 1800s to combat the insect pests that did exist. Despite this fact, the insect problem seems to have worsened. In 1944, a work written by one of America's top experts on fruit growing indicated that more than twenty insects were causing trouble for apple growers. Today, bulletins issued by the United States Department of Agriculture list more than thirty insects that feed on apples.

Why does the insect problem seem to be getting worse? Apples today are bigger and sweeter than their earlier cousins. These qualities may make them a more desirable food to a greater number of insect pests. Too, apples today are mostly grown in huge orchards. These orchards add up to big hunks of bug bait. Once America's insects learned to include apples in their diets, they became a problem and this state of affairs has remained ever since.

* * *

In addition to being a source of food for centuries, the apple has also been a source of folklore. One of the most popular American myths is about Johnny Appleseed. The folk tales about Johnny Appleseed are based on a man named John Chapman who lived on the Ohio-Indiana frontier. He was a strange but pleasant fellow who enjoyed his liquor and loved plants and animals. He spent his time planting apple seeds, which he obtained from cider mills.

One of the people who helped to create the myth of Johnny Appleseed was a woman named Rosella Rice who knew Chapman when she was a youngster living in Ohio. When she grew up she wrote about him. But instead of writing about him exactly as she remembered him, she used her imagination to transform him from an odd and colorful fellow into an American saint— Johnny Appleseed. The information about Johnny Appleseed which follows is taken from her stories.

She describes Johnny as having long hair and a long beard and dressing oddly in old clothes which he received in exchange for his work— planting apple seeds. Sometimes he carried a bag or two of seeds on an old horse. But more often he bore them on his back, going from place to place on the wild frontier, clearing a little patch, surrounding it with a crudely made fence and planting seeds therein. He had little orchards all through Pennsylvania, Ohio, and Indiana.

According to Rice, Johnny was never known to hunt any animal or to give any animal pain. One time, when overtaken by night while traveling, he crawled into a hollow log and slept till morning. In the other end of the log were a bear and her cubs. Johnny said he knew the bear would not hurt him, and that there was room enough for all.

The Indians liked Johnny and treated him very kindly. They regarded him as a man above his fellows. He could endure pain like an Indian warrior; he could thrust pins into his flesh without a shiver. Indeed, he could endure pain so well that his way of treating a wound or sore was to sear it with a hot iron and then treat it as a burn.

In 1838 according to legend, Johnny, who was then well on in years, decided to head further west to escape the villages that were springing up. Stagecoaches loaded with travelers were common; schools were being built; and brick houses were taking the place of lowly cabins.

During the next few years, he returned to Indiana several times. The last time was in the year he died, 1845. One day in the spring of that year, he visited a friend in western Indiana. The friend, as usual, greeted him warmly. That evening, Johnny refused to eat anything except some bread and milk which he had while sitting on the doorstep and looking out on the setting sun. The next morning, when a physician came to the house to examine Johnny, he saw that Johnny, near death, was perfectly calm and peaceful. His life had been filled with unselfishness. His memory would live on, and his deeds would live anew every spring in the apple blossoms he loved so well.

1 **About the Reading.** Put the letter of the correct answer on the line to the left.

_(b)_ 1. In the American colonies, the major use of apples was for _____ .

    (a) brandy   (c) fritters

    (b) cider   (d) puddings

_(b)_ 2. Cider vinegar was important to the colonists because _____ .

    (a) it could be used to make brandy

    (b) it enabled them to preserve fruits and vegetables

    (c) it was something to drink when cider was not available

    (d) it was the major source of medicine

_(c)_ 3. A main reason that the apple was especially popular in early American cooking was that _____ .

    (a) an apple a day keeps the doctor away

    (b) apple orchards were common in New England

    (c) it could be stored for a long period of time

    (d) it tasted good in many different types of dishes

_(a)_ 4. As farms and villages replaced the forests, one of the effects mentioned by the author was _____ .

    (a) farmers were confronted with an increasingly difficult insect problem

    (b) consumers began to prefer canned goods to preserved fruits and vegetables

    (c) folk tales such as Johnny Appleseed became popular because people wished to remember "the good old days"

    (d) people no longer had to drink cider so much because drinking water became increasingly pure

_(d)_ 5. Which of the following is *not* cited as a possible cause of the increasing problem apple growers are experiencing with insects?

    (a) Apples today are larger than apples of years ago.

    (b) Apples today are sweeter than apples of years ago.

    (c) Because apple trees are grown in orchards rather than scattered about the countryside, insects find it easy to attack the trees.

    (d) Foreign insects do not have trouble adapting to American varieties of apples.

_(a)_   6. The folk tales about Johnny Appleseed are based on the life of _____ .

       (a) John Chapman   (c) Rosella Rice

       (b) Peter Wynne   (d) E. P. Dutton

_(c)_   7. The folk tales about Johnny Appleseed tell of his _____ .

       (a) hunting and fishing trips

       (b) trying to make a name for himself

       (c) planting apple orchards throughout Ohio, Pennsylvania, and Indiana

       (d) friendship with Rosella Rice

_(b)_   8. According to the folk tales, the Indians admired Johnny Appleseed for his _____ .

       (a) compassion   (c) honesty

       (b) courage   (d) resourcefulness

_(a)_   9. Based on the information in this reading passage, which of the following does *not* describe Johnny Appleseed as portrayed in Rosella Rice's tales?

       (a) a drinking man   (c) a man of daring

       (b) a lover of nature   (d) a wanderer

_(d)_   10. According to Rosella Rice, Johnny thought his memory would live on because _____ .

       (a) his children would continue to tell stories about him

       (b) he believed that his diary would someday be published

       (c) he knew Rosella Rice's stories about him would continue to be popular

       (d) the apple trees he planted would continue to grow and remind people of him

2 **A Recipe for Apple Fritters.** Read the recipe for apple fritters and then answer the questions which follow.

Aplyn Fruturs

For to mak Fruturs: Nym flowre and eyryn and grynd peper and mak therto a batour and par aplyn and kyt hem to brode penys and cast hem theryn and fry hem in batour wyth fresch grees and serve it forthe.

Did you have any trouble reading this recipe? Believe it or not, this is English—English as it was spoken and written from about 1125 to about 1475.

1. List five words from the recipe that are the same now as they were during the 1125–1475 period of history.

   flowre (for)   cast   fry   serve   in

2. Study the recipe and then match the words on the right with their modern spellings.

   batter   _take_   A. nym
   broad
   cut   _eggs_   B. eyryn
   eggs   _batter_   C. batour (flower mixer)
   grease
   pare   _pare_   D. par
   take   _cut_   E. kyt
   them   _them_   F. hem
             broad   G. brode brɔːd (麺のたぐい)
             grease   H. grees

3. Study the recipe and then write the modern English spellings for these words.

   A. fruturs   _fritters_
   B. flowre   _flower (ur)_
   C. peper   _pepper_
   D. mak   _make_
   E. penys   _pennies pieces_
   F. fresch   _fresh_

4. Most modern recipes give measurements. For example, a modern recipe might tell you to use 1 cup flour. Why do you think measurements were not used in very old recipes?

① Immigrants came from many countries, and their measurements were not the same. ② They didn't have measurements

5. Do you think the English we speak and write will be as strange to English-speaking people living five hundred years from now as the English in the recipe is to us? Give reasons to support your opinion.

Yes. Languages are changeable. We sometimes make new words because new things are made or discovered.

3   Words with More Than One Meaning. Each of the underlined words in the sentences below has more than one meaning. Check the meaning which applies to the word as it has been used in the sentence.

1. "The apple was made into pies and fritters and puddings—a host of dishes."

   _____ an army

   _____ a living thing that harbors and provides food for another living thing

   __✓__ a great number

   __✗__ one who entertains guests

2. After three-year-old Linda had been examined in the emergency room, she was moved to the children's ward.

   _____ a large room in a hospital usually holding six or more patients

   _____ a section of a city or a town

   __✓__ a section of a hospital for the care of a particular group of patients

   _____ any person under the protection or care of another

3. The governor's staff worked round the clock to have the budget review prepared in time for the upcoming television debate.

   __✓__ a group of assistants or workers

   _____ a pole upon which a flag is displayed

   _____ a stick, rod, or cane carried as an aid in walking

   _____ in music, a set of lines and their spaces upon which notes are written or printed

4. When the union boss polled the workers, he was surprised to learn that their main complaints had nothing at all to do with money.

   _____ to cast a vote or ballot

   __✓__ to question a sample group of people in order to survey public opinion

   _____ to trim or cut off hair, wool, or horns

5. The Quincys decided to purchase the Southern mansion despite the retired caretaker's warnings that spirits had walked its marbled floors since as far back as the Civil War.

   __✓__ ghosts

   _____ liquor

   __✗__ one's mood or emotional state

6. As Doc Parker dabbed ointment on the sobbing gunfighter's forehead, he said, "Don't carry on so, Matt. You know as well as I do that the bullet only grazed you."

   _____ to feed on growing grasses

   _____ to put livestock out to feed

   __✓__ to touch lightly in passing; to skim or brush

7. An annoyed English gentleman once asked, "What business have people to get children to <u>plague</u> their neighbors?"

    ____ a disease which is usually deadly

    ____ a sudden occurrence which usually causes destruction

    __✓_ to annoy or upset

8. Of Helen, a figure in Greek mythology whose remarkable beauty caused men to start a war, an English poet wrote, "Was this the face that <u>launched</u> a thousand ships?"

    ____ any large, open motorboat

    __✓_ to put into action

    __≠_ to hurl or throw

9. James Whistler felt honored when, in 1891, the Society of British Artists purchased a <u>canvas</u> he had titled "The Artist's Mother."

    ____ a heavy material used for making tents and sails

    __✓_ a piece of such a material on which a painting is made, especially an oil painting

    ____ the floor of a ring in which boxing or wrestling takes place

10. An English writer once said, "Wrong opinions and practices slowly <u>yield</u> to fact and argument."

    __✓_ to give way to what is stronger or better

    ____ to furnish or give a return

    ____ the profit obtained from an investment

4 **The Suffix -*tion*.** Use the words at the left to complete this exercise correctly.

accommodations (設備)   *accommodations*   1. what a hotel offers

addiction (常用癖)   *reservation*   2. what a traveler makes to get an airline ticket

combination

compositions   *starvation*   3. what being without food can cause

definitions

exhaustion (情況·疲勞)   *investigations*   4. what commissions and detectives conduct

explanations

extractions (拔出)   *inflation*   5. what consumers always complain about

graduation   *extractions*   6. what dentists perform

infections (感染)

inflation   *definitions*   7. what the dictionary contains

investigations   *addiction*   8. what drug abuse can lead to

reservation

starvation (飢餓)   *compositions*   9. what English students write

temptation   *infection*   10. what insect bites can cause

        exhaustion   11. what overwork can lead to

        explanations   12. what parents often demand when their children come home late

        temptation   13. what sinners are warned not to give in to

        graduation   14. what students look forward to

        combination   15. what you might need to know to open a locker or safe

5 **Using the Apostrophe with Plural Words.** *Plural*, if you remember, means *more than one*. For example, one apple, two apples. *Apples* is the plural form of *apple*. When the plural form of a word ends in *s*, add just the apostrophe to show ownership. Study the two examples carefully, and then write the plural form of ownership for the following.

1. the growth of the colonies   the colonies' growth

2. the defense of the players   the players' defense

3. the pranks of the rascals   the rascals' pranks

4. the construction of the skyscrapers   the skyscrapers' construction

5. the ripeness of the bananas   the bananas' ripeness

6. the dismissal of the cartoonists   the cartoonists' dismissal

7. the friendliness of the Canadians   the Canadians' friendliness

8. the red glare of the rockets   the rockets' red glare

9. the entertainment of the visitors   the visitors' entertainment

10. the boldness of the daredevils   the daredevils' boldness

11. the roar of the motors   the motors' roar

12. the availability of the nurses   the nurses' availability

6 **The Unfruitful Reunion.** Use the fruits listed below to complete the rather unusual dialogue that follows. Your imagination, a good dictionary and, perhaps, the help of a fellow student should help you figure out the correct answers.

apple	fig いちじく	lime	prune
banana	fruitcake	Mulberry (桑の実)	raspberry
Cherry	grape	peach	rhubarb [ruːbɑːb] (タイオう)
date	lemon	plum	strawberry

The Unfruitful Reunion

Scene: A seafood restaurant. Luella enters breathlessly, surveys the room, and sees Emory, her

ex-husband and ___dates___ for the evening, seated at a corner table.

Luella: Sorry I'm late. So how's your new van running? I heard through the

___grape___ vine that you got yourself stuck with a first-class ___lemon___ .

Emory: That it is. Runs like a leftover from World War II.

Luella: I tried to tell you a hundred times that no one in his right mind would give a

___fig___ for that pile of junk.
     (I don't care)

Emory: Skip the insulting reminders. I want to know what on earth happened to your hair. What
     (Don't tell me the stupid)
caused you to confuse the shampoo with a ketchup bottle?

Luella: Now who's being insulting? *(After a pause)* Well, er, I told the girl at the style shop I wanted

it ___strawberry___ -blond; and, uh, well, I guess she kind of went overboard.

Emory: Overboard! Honey, she sank and took you down with her. You might look strange, but you're

still a ___peach___ of a woman, Luella. Are you going to order your usual

___Cherry___ -stone Clam Delight?

Luella: Oh, Emory! You can be so sweet when you want. Just like my dear daddy who used to

always tell me I was the ___apple___ of his eye!

Emory: *(His expression changes swiftly from delight to pain—as if he's just slipped on a*
     banana
___lemon___ *peel.)* Now, don't be an old ___prune___ , Luella. You know I
                                                          (dry)
can't stand it when you bring up the subject of your dear, deceased daddy.

Luella: Seeing that it would be ill-mannered to have a ___rhubarb___ right here in the middle

of the restaurant, I shall agree with everything you say and not mention my darling father

again.

Emory: The way you always want the _lime_ light I'm surprised you're not throwing the silverware at me just to get some attention.

Luella: *(Hotly)* I swear, Emory, you're as nutty as a _fruitcake_ !

Emory: Now calm down sugar_plum_ . Your face is starting to look like your hair.

Luella: You know, trying to have an adult discussion with you is as childish as playing "Here We Go Round the _Mulberry_ Bush"!

Emory: *(Angrily)* That's it! I've had enough! *(He stands, delivers a loud _raspberry_ to his ex-wife, and storms out as the other diners stare at him in disbelief.)*

The End

Lesson 17

Save Your Stomach

Words for Study

mysterious	navel	fraying	macaroni
converted	centuries	insert	diarrhea
digestive	famous	dissolved	constipation
population	Alexis St. Martin	cereal	laxatives
annoyance	Beaumont	miracle	calories
functions	science	typical	medium

Save Your Stomach

The most mysterious part of the universe for many of us is not some faraway planet, the ocean floor, or anything else removed from us. It is the long, churning world within us. Call it the gut, belly, middle, or stomach, if explorers discovered such a thing on one of their adventuresome voyages, it would be a source of great wonder.

In just one year, more than half a ton of food is minced, extracted, and converted in the stomach. The stomach takes care of our food, but it also disturbs and worries us. It is generally accepted that 60 per cent of adult patients who seek assistance from their doctors have complaints involving their digestive system. One-sixth of all major illnesses involve the gut. Each year five million people spend some time in a hospital for stomach disorders. One-half the population of the United States complains about something wrong with their digestive systems.

Yet the stomach has received little public attention. Except in advertisements, the growl of a stomach can hardly compete for prime TV time with the thump of a heart. Digestive disorders are usually defined as a source of discomfort and annoyance rather than as life-threatening situations. Very little has been done to help the public understand how the stomach functions.

In fact, most people don't even know where the stomach is. Many people think the stomach is on a level with the navel, or bellybutton. Commonly, however, the stomach is at rib level with its upper end just below the heart. Another false concept shared by many people is that all stomachs are pretty much alike in shape. Not so. Where in some people the stomach is held up high with no part of it falling below the level of the ribs; in others, part of it dips a little or a lot below, even in some cases coming close to the groin area.

For centuries, of course, nothing was known about the stomach's role in the process of digestion. In the late eighteenth century, a famous English physician declared, "Some doctors say the stomach is a Mill; others that it is a Vat; others that it is a Stew Pan; but in my view of the matter it is neither a Mill, a Vat, nor a Stew Pan—but a Stomach." No one knew exactly what the English doctor meant, which may have been why his fame vastly increased.

The truth would have to await a shotgun accident in a trader's store in Canada in June, 1822, in which the blast tore off the skin and muscles of the upper part of Alexis St. Martin's abdomen and, in addition, the outer layer of the wall of his stomach. On being called to help, the best that Dr. William Beaumont, a young United States Army doctor, could do was to stitch the stomach edges to the skin.

Happily, for himself and for science, St. Martin lived with a hole in his stomach. With his consent, Dr. Beaumont could look in the hole and see the stomach move. He could also see digestive juice oozing onto the stomach lining. He could lower into the stomach a piece of meat on a string, pull it out half an hour later and see a bit of fraying at the meat edges; insert it again for another half hour and pull it out to find half the meat gone; reinsert it for another hour whereupon it was gone, completely dissolved.

St. Martin's stomach peephole also enabled Dr. Beaumont to discover that the juice which dissolved the food appeared only when food was being chewed or when it entered the stomach. About a century later, another American doctor discovered that this juice flowed plentifully when a person smelled something he liked to eat, but dried up when the food neither smelled nor looked good. This could be why good cooking is so valued: everything else being equal, the better you like the food, the better you can digest it.

The human stomach can hold about a quart and a half of food with no sense of discomfort. Food tends to remain in the stomach three to four hours but will stay there longer if the meal is high in fat. On the other hand, a meal which mainly consists of starch tends to empty more quickly out of the stomach. Thus, you can expect to become hungry again sooner after a breakfast of juice, cereal, toast, and tea than after one of bacon, eggs, and milk.

Speaking of breakfast, one is reminded of the pride Americans take in the expression, "three square meals a day." Is there any truth in this expression? The Germans also have an expression: *Der Mensch ist was er isst*—Man is what he eats. If the German expression is correct, it is a miracle that the number of Americans suffering from stomach disorders is not even higher.

In 1974, Dr. Paul A. Fine conducted a study which pointed out the difference between how Americans think they eat and how they actually do eat. The study showed that the typical American mother described her family's eating pattern as three square meals a day with after-school snacks for the children. But when Fine's researchers asked housewives to record the food their families actually ate, the eating pattern was indeed something else.

Three out of four families do not eat breakfast together and many eat no breakfast at all. As for eating dinner together, it can take place "as seldom as three days a week or less" and may often take only twenty minutes to eat. Snacking is the pattern of Americans from early morning to bedtime, and even then it does not end. "People cannot sleep—they are restless—they are hungry. They get up and raid the leftovers they would not eat at dinner."

This means there is an average of about twenty "food contacts" a day in the family instead of three square meals. The "American mainstream," Dr. Fine reported, feeds on "Oreos, peanut butter, Crisco, TV dinners, cake mix, macaroni and cheese, Pepsi and Coke, pizzas, Jell-O, hamburgers, Rice-a-Roni, Spaghetti-O's, pork and beans, ketchup, and instant coffee."

It is not just the quality of the food we put in our stomachs that can cause mild upsets and serious disorders. Many studies have revealed that our emotions can affect our stomach's ability to function. Let's say that you often feel angry or resentful. These emotions cause the stomach juices to flow more freely with the result that the food is out of the stomach in less than its normal time, and you may suffer from diarrhea. On the other hand, if you are often sad, fearful, or depressed, the food remains in the stomach undigested for many hours, and the result is constipation.

Given the fact that Americans spend more than $350 million each year for laxatives and other medicines created to give our stomachs comfort, it would be well worth our time to learn more about our stomachs and good eating habits. It is both tragic and remarkable that problems such as diarrhea, constipation, indigestion, gas, and heartburn have come to be defined as features of normal living by many individuals who are convinced they're in good health. The truth is—they're not enjoying good health at all.

Adapted from *Save Your Stomach* by Lawrence Galton, 1977. Reprinted by permission of Crown Publishers, Inc.

According to the Author. Listed below are fourteen details cited by the author to support statements he has made in the reading passage. Match *twelve* of these details with the statements they support. Look back at the passage if you need help. The first one has been done to get you started.

Supporting Details

✓ Many people eat no breakfast at all.
✓ Many people believe all stomachs look alike.
  Alexis St. Martin was shot in the abdomen.
✓ Raiding the refrigerator in the middle of the night is common.
✓ Constipation can be the result of depression.
✓ One-sixth of all major illnesses are related to stomach disorders.
✓ Many people think the stomach is located on a level with the navel.
✓ Meals high in starch tend to empty out of the stomach more quickly.
  Stomach problems should be expected to occur in modern society.
✓ One-half the population complains about their digestive systems.
✓ Diarrhea can be the result of anger.
✓ More than $350 million is spent each year on stomach medicine.
  Meals high in fat tend to empty out of the stomach more slowly.
✓ Americans average about twenty "food contacts" a day.

Statements

1. Generally speaking, people know very little about the stomach.

   a. _Many people believe all stomachs look alike._

   b. _Many people think the stomach is located on a level with the navel._

2. The stomach is a major source of health problems in the United States.

   a. _One-sixth of all major illnesses are related to stomach disorders._

   b. _One-half the population complains about their digestive systems._

   c. _More than $350 million is spent each year on stomach medicine._

3. The three-square-meals-a-day eating pattern is largely a myth.

   a. _Raiding the refrigerator in the middle of the night is common._

   b. _Many people eat no breakfast at all._

   c. _Americans average about twenty "food contacts" a day._

4. What you eat affects your digestion.

   a. _Meals high in starch tend to empty out of the stomach more quickly._

   b. _Meals high in fat tend to empty out of the stomach more slowly._

5. How you feel affects your digestion.

   a. _Constipation can be the result of depression._

   b. _Diarrhea can be the result of anger._

2 Word Review. Underline the word in each line that best relates to the first word. Study the example before you begin.

1. **ocean:** Red   Huron   <u>Pacific</u>   Mediterranean

2. **gadabout:** warrior   villager   youngster   wanderer

3. **eagerness:** camel   beaver   gopher   peacock

4. **debt:** CIA   FBI   IOU   IRS

5. **stomach:** coma   ulcer   cornea   itchiness

6. **disease:** mumps   heartburn   pimples   freckles

7. **orchard:** bananas   rhubarb   cherries   watermelons

8. **adder:** hiss   bleat   graze   gallop

9. **artist:** easel   profit   applause   signature

10. **soldier:** chuckhole   pothole   peephole   foxhole

11. **satellite:** moon   star   meteor   planet

12. **fuel:** water   mealtime   oil   cell

13. **19th century:** 1700s   1800s   1900s   2000s

14. **greed:** Aesop   Pan   Apollo   Midas

15. **frayed:** ragged   hardened   dissolved   imprisoned

3 The Suffix -sion. Use the words listed below to complete the sentences.

admission confusion intermission profession
commission decision invasion revision
conclusion division omission supervision
concussion extension permission transfusion
confession impression possession transmission

1. After his ninth explanation of the difference between long and short _____division_____ during the arithmetic lesson, Norman wondered why he had ever considered teaching to be a worthy _____~~confusion~~ profession_____

2. Because the teenager was a minor, he was not able to receive the necessary blood _____transfusion_____ until the doctor had obtained _____permission_____ from one of his parents.

3. Having completed their survey, the _____commission_____ appointed by the governor to study eating patterns came to the sad _____conclusion_____ that people would rather complain about their health than actually do anything about it.

4. In the mass _____~~omission~~ confusion_____ during the fire drill, Dave lost his prize _____possession_____, a pocket watch which his uncle had given him for his birthday.

5. Mr. Kelly was under the _____impression_____ that the carpenters would have the _____~~profession~~ extension_____ he was adding to the left wing of his mansion completed in time for his daughter's wedding, but he was wrong.

6. "Now I've heard everything!" exclaimed the English teacher when one of her students explained that he had not completed the _____revision_____ of the composition because, while doing his homework, he had tapped his pencil on his head so often that he was now suffering from a mild _____concussion_____.

7. The evening after the advertisement appeared in the newspaper announcing that the price of _____admission_____ had been reduced to one dollar, there was such an _____invasion_____ of eager moviegoers that the manager had to turn hundreds of disappointed people away.

8. The organist was so upset over the _____~~extension~~ omission_____ of his name from the concert program that he stormed out of the theater during the _____intermission_____.

162   Lesson 17

9. Under the _supervision_ of the tough, new chief of detectives, the investigating team finally got Molly Monroe to sign a _confession_ in spite of her claim that she was just an innocent victim of circumstances.

10. When the man at Solly's Garage told Ms. Hood that her station wagon needed a brand-new _transmission_, she was confronted with the _decision_ about whether to have the car fixed or shop around for a new one.

4 **Using the Apostrophe with Plural Words.** Write the plural form of possession for the following. Review the examples in Lesson 16 before you begin.

1. the recipes of the chefs _the chefs' recipes_
2. the output of the steel mills _the steel mills' output_
3. the thoughtlessness of the litterbugs _the litterbugs' thoughtlessness_
4. the settlement of the strikers _the strikers' settlement_
5. the saddles of the cowpunchers _the cowpunchers' saddles_
6. the distrust of the villagers _the villagers' distrust_
7. the possessions of the roommates _the roommates' possessions_
8. the beauty of the mountains _the mountains' beauty_
9. the findings of the researchers _the researchers' findings_
10. the affection of the sweethearts _the sweethearts' affection_

5   **Counting Calories.** In the beginning, calories had nothing at all to do with food. A calorie was simply a unit of heat used in the study of physics. In the late 1800s, however, someone came up with the idea of measuring food in calories, and we've been counting (or thinking maybe we should be counting) calories ever since. Use the chart below to answer the questions which follow.

Calorie Chart			
Food	Calories	Food	Calories
Applesauce, sweetened, ½ cup	127	French toast, 1 piece	170
Applesauce, unsweetened, ½ cup	50	Frog legs, fried, 2 large	140
Bacon, 1 crisp 6″ strip	45	Honey, 1 tablespoon	65
Banana, 1 medium-sized	100	Ice cream, store-bought, plain, ½ cup	125–165
Beans, baked, canned, ½ cup	155	Jam or jelly, 1 tablespoon	50–60
Beans, green or snap, ½ cup cooked	15	Lettuce, 6 large leaves	30
Beef, 1 hamburger, 3-oz. patty	185–245	Macaroni, cooked, plain, ½ cup	80
Beer, 12 oz.	150	Macaroni and cheese, ½ cup	215
Bread, store-bought, white, 1 slice, ½″ thick	60–65	Marshmallows, 5	125
Bread, store-bought, whole-wheat, 1 slice, ½″ thick	60	Mayonnaise, 1 tablespoon	65
Butter, 1 square, ¼″ thick	70	Milk, skimmed, 1 cup	90
Cake, chocolate layer, 2″ square	356	Milk, whole fresh, 1 cup	160
Carrots, ½ cup, cooked	25	Orange juice, 1 cup	110
Chicken, broiler, small	136	Pancake, 1, 4″ diameter	60
Chicken, fried, ½ breast	155	Peanut butter, 2 tablespoons	190
Chicken potpie, 1 individual pie, 4 ¼″ diameter	535	Pineapple, canned, 1 slice with juice	78
Chocolate, 1 cup made with milk	245–277	Pineapple, fresh, ½ cup diced	40
Chocolate bar, milk, 1 oz.	145	Popcorn, 1 cup, no butter	25
Chocolate malted milk, made with 8 oz. milk and ice cream	502	Potato chips, 8 to 10 large	100
Coffee, clear, 1 cup	0	Pretzels, 5 small sticks	5
Coffee with 1 tablespoon cream, 1 cup	30	Shredded wheat, 1 large biscuit	100
Coffee with 1 lump sugar, 1 cup	27	Spaghetti, plain, cooked, 1 cup	155
Cooky, 1 sugar, 3″ diameter	64	Tea, clear, unsweetened, 1 cup	0
Corn flakes, ¾ cup	75	Tomato, fresh, 1, 3″ diameter	40
Doughnut, cake-type, plain, 1	165	Tomato juice, 1 cup	50
Doughnut, sugared, 1	180	Tomato soup, cream homemade, 1 cup	175
Egg, 1 fried with 1 teaspoon butter	105	Tuna fish, canned, water packed, ½ cup	165
Egg, 1 scrambled with 2 tablepoons milk and 1 teaspoon butter	110	Tuna fish, canned in oil, 3 oz.	170
		Turkey, roast, dark meat, 3 ½ oz.	203
Egg, 1 whole, boiled or poached	80	Turkey, roast, light meat, 3 ½ oz.	176
		Vegetable juice, 1 cup	48
		Vegetable soup, 1 cup	80
		Yogurt, whole milk, ½ cup	75

1. For what unit of measurement is *oz.* the abbreviation? *Weight.*

2. For what unit of measurement is " the symbol? *Length.*

3. How many calories are there in one marshmallow? *25 calories.*

4. How many calories are there in one large leaf of lettuce? *5 calories.*

5. Cite one example from the calorie chart which indicates that raw foods can be lower in calories than canned foods.

   ~~Green beans~~ of 1/2 cup contain 15 calories and canned beans do 155 calories

6. Cite two examples from the calorie chart which indicate that, if you are dieting, sugar is something you want to avoid.

   Cake, chocolate layer, 2" square contains 356 calories and a doughnut, sugared 180 calories.

7. What from the chart would you choose to drink each day if you needed to gain a few pounds in order to make first-string tackle on the football team?

   Chocolate malted milk, made with 8 oz. milk and ice cream.

8. Describe the kind of sandwich you would make for yourself for lunch if you were trying to lose weight.

   I'll make sandwich with lettuce, tomato and water packed tuna fish.

9. In the reading passage, you learned that foods high in starch tend to empty more quickly out of the stomach than foods high in fats. Prepare two breakfast menus—one high in starch and the other high in fats. You may refer to the reading passage for suggestions.

High Starch Breakfast		High Fat Breakfast	
Food	# of Calories	Food	# of Calories
Tea, clear, unsweetened, 1 cup	*0*	*Egg, 1 scrambled with 2 tablespoons milk and 1 teaspoon butter*	*110*
		Bacon 1 crisp 6" strip	*45*
Corn flakes 3/4 cup	*75*	*French toast, 1 piece*	*170*
Yogurt whole milk 1/2 cup	*75*	*Milk, whole fresh, 1 cup*	*160*

According to your menus, is there a tradeoff between not becoming hungry soon after breakfast and the number of calories consumed? Explain.

If I tradeoff between corn flakes with yogurt and French toast, there is not big difference about calories.

10. **Which is more important to you—eating what you want, or eating what your body requires for good health? Be sure to offer some reasons for your answer.**

Eating what my body requires for good health is more
important. For example I like cake, but if I continue
to eat a lot of cake, I'll [develop] get diabetes. We should
think of the valance of nutrition.

Lesson 18

A Breakfast Scene

Words for Study

Tribune	pajamas	viciously	masculine
maximum	utensils	mechanically	masculinity
indifference	gleefully	unnaturally	polisher
Colonel McCormick	exasperated	oppression	sausages
automatic	outraged	frustration	possessive
emphasis	abruptly	comically	necessarily

A Breakfast Scene

In the last lesson, you read that many American families don't eat breakfast together. In this lesson, you will read a scene from a famous American play entitled *A Raisin in the Sun* which offers us a picture of one American family at breakfast.

Walter: Something the matter with you this morning?

Ruth: No—I'm just sleepy as the devil. What kind of eggs you want?

Walter: Not scrambled. *(Ruth starts to scramble eggs.)* Paper come? *(Ruth points impatiently to the rolled up Tribune on the table, and he gets it and spreads it out and vaguely reads the front page.)* Set off another bomb yesterday.

Ruth: *(Maximum indifference)* Did they?

Walter: *(Looking up)* What's the matter with you?

Ruth: Ain't nothing the matter with me. And don't keep asking me that this morning.

Walter: Ain't nobody bothering you. *(Reading the news of the day absently again)* Say Colonel McCormick is sick.

Ruth: *(Affecting tea-party interest)* Is he now? Poor thing.

Walter: *(Sighing and looking at his watch)* Oh, me. *(He waits)* Now what is that boy doing in that bathroom all this time? He just going to have to start getting up earlier. I can't be being late to work on account of him fooling around in there.

Ruth: *(Turning on him)* Oh, no he ain't going to be getting up no earlier no such thing! It ain't his fault that he can't get to bed no earlier nights 'cause he got a bunch of crazy good-for-nothing clowns sitting up running their mouths in what is supposed to be his bedroom after ten o'clock at night...

Walter: That's what you mad about, ain't it? The things I want to talk about with my friends just couldn't be important in your mind, could they?

(He rises and finds a cigarette in her handbag on the table and crosses to the little window and looks out, smoking and deeply enjoying this first one.)

Ruth: *(Almost matter-of-factly, a complaint too automatic to deserve emphasis)* Why you always got to smoke before you eat in the morning?

Walter: *(At the window)* Just look at 'em down there...Running and racing to work...*(He turns and faces his wife and watches her a moment at the stove, and then, suddenly)* You look young this morning, baby.

Ruth: *(Indifferently)* Yeah?

Walter: Just for a second—stirring them eggs. It's gone now—just for a second it was—you looked real young again. *(Then, drily)* It's gone now—you look like yourself again.

Ruth: Man, if you don't shut up and leave me alone.

Walter: *(Looking out to the street again)* First thing a man ought to learn in life is not to make love to no colored woman first thing in the morning. You all some evil people at eight o'clock in the morning.

(Travis appears in the hall doorway, almost fully dressed and quite wide awake now, his towels and pajamas across his shoulders. He opens the door and signals for his father to make for the bathroom in a hurry.)

Travis: *(Watching the bathroom)* Daddy, come on!

(Walter gets his bathroom utensils and flies out to the bathroom.)

Ruth: Sit down and have your breakfast, Travis.

Travis: Mama, this is Friday. *(Gleefully)* Check coming tomorrow, huh?

Ruth: You get your mind off money and eat your breakfast.

Travis: *(Eating)* This is the morning we supposed to bring fifty cents to school.

Ruth: Well, I ain't got no fifty cents this morning.

Travis: Teacher say we have to.

Ruth: I don't care what teacher say. I ain't got it. Eat your breakfast, Travis.

Travis: I am eating.

Ruth: Hush up now and just eat!

(The boy gives her an exasperated look for

her lack of understanding, and eats grudgingly.)*

Travis: You think Grandmama would have it?

Ruth: No! And I want you to stop asking your grandmother for money, you hear me?

Travis: *(Outraged)* Gaaaleee! I don't ask her, she just gimme it sometimes!

Ruth: Travis Willard Younger—I got too much on me this morning to be—

Travis: Maybe Daddy—

Ruth: Travis!

(The boy hushes abruptly. They are both quiet and tense for several seconds.)

Travis: *(Presently)* Could I maybe go carry some groceries in front of the supermarket for a little while after school then?

Ruth: Just hush, I said. *(Travis jabs his spoon into his cereal bowl viciously, and rests his head in anger upon his fists.)* If you through eating, you can get over there and make up your bed. *(The boy obeys stiffly and crosses the room, almost mechanically, to the bed and more or less carefully folds the covering. He carries the bedding into his mother's room and returns with his books and cap.)*

Travis: *(Sulking and standing apart from her unnaturally)* I'm gone.

Ruth: *(Looking up from the stove to inspect him automatically)* Come here. *(He crosses to her and she studies his head.)* If you don't take this comb and fix this here head, you better! *(Travis puts down his books with a great sigh of oppression, and crosses to the mirror. His mother mutters under her breath about his "stubbornness".)* 'Bout to march out of here with that head looking just like chickens slept in it! I just don't know where you get your stubborn ways...And get your jacket, too. Looks chilly out this morning.

Travis: *(With conspicuously brushed hair and jacket)* I'm gone.

Ruth: Get carfare and milk money—*(Waving one finger)*—and not a single penny for no caps, you hear me?

Travis: *(With sullen politeness)* Yes'm.

(He turns in outrage to leave. His mother watches after him as in his frustration he approaches the door almost comically. When she speaks to him, her voice has become a very gentle tease.)

Ruth: *(Mocking; as she thinks he would say it)*

Oh, Mama makes me so mad sometimes, I don't know what to do! *(She waits and continues to his back as he stands stock-still in front of the door.)* I wouldn't kiss that woman good-bye for nothing in this world this morning! *(The boy finally turns around and rolls his eyes at her, knowing the mood has changed and he is vindicated; he does not, however, move toward her yet.)* Not for nothing in this world! *(She finally laughs aloud at him and holds out her arms to him and we see that it is a way between them, very old and practiced. He crosses to her and allows her to embrace him warmly but keeps his face fixed with masculine rigidity. She holds him back from her presently and looks at him and runs her fingers over the features of his face. With utter gentleness.)* Now— whose little old angry man are you?

Travis: *(The masculinity and gruffness start to fade at last)* Aw gaalee, Mama...

Ruth: *(Mimicking)* Aw-gaaaaalleeeee, Mama! *(She pushes him, with rough playfulness and finality, toward the door)* Get on out of here or you going to be late.

1   About the Scene. Answer the following questions in good sentence form.

1. Describe Ruth's relationship with her husband Walter. Be sure to include details from the scene to support your description.

   They don't have good relationship. Walter said Ruth looked young, but she didn't like to hear it.

2. Describe Ruth's relationship with her son Travis. Be sure to include details from the scene to support your description.

   They love each other. Travis was very angry because Ruth was luck of understanding about giving him money. But finally "The masculinity and gruffness start to fade at last".

3. Imagine that you are the director of *A Raisin in the Sun*. Describe the type of actress you would be looking for to play the part of Ruth.

   She is a middle aged and a little bit lovely lady, but is just interested in her child insted of her husband.

4. "A Breakfast Scene" is taken from the first act of *A Raisin in the Sun*, which is a three-act play. Based on what you've read, do you think Walter and Ruth will live "happily ever after," or do you think their marriage will fall apart? Again, include details and reasons to explain your answer.

   They will not fall apart but live unhappily. Because Walter loves Ruth, but Ruth doesn't. She will live with Walter just for taking care of her son.

2 **Synonyms and Antonyms.** Choose a synonym to fill in the first blank in each sentence. Choose an antonym to fill in the second blank. Study the example before you begin.

Synonyms

√affection	extract
√average	√gleeful
∪broad	√introduction
√comical	∪masculine
∪exasperated	∪minimum
√extend	√sudden

Antonyms

√compress	√insert
√conclusion	∪maximum
∪contented	∪narrow
dejected	∪remarkable
√dislike	∪slow
√feminine	√tragic

1. Beginning and _introduction_ are antonyms for _conclusion_.
2. Abrupt and _sudden_ are antonyms for _slow_.
3. Fondness and _affection_ are antonyms for _dislike_.
4. Frustrated and _exasperated_ are antonyms for _contented_.
5. Funny and _comical_ are antonyms for _tragic_.
6. Least and _minimum_ are antonyms for _maximum_.
7. Lengthen and _extend_ are antonyms for _compress_.
8. Manly and _masculine_ are antonyms for _feminine_.
9. Merry and _gleeful_ are antonyms for _dejected_.
10. Remove and _extract_ are antonyms for _insert_.
11. Typical and _average_ are antonyms for _remarkable_.
12. Wide and _broad_ are antonyms for _narrow_.

Food for Thought. Foods and sources of food have given our language many interesting slang terms and expressions. Use your common sense and imagination to answer the following questions. The dictionary may be of help to you for some of these terms and expressions.

_(c)_ 1. Which of the following is known for being a brainy person who has many ideas?

   (a) bonehead   (b) cabbage head   (c) egghead   (d) meathead

_(d)_ 2. When the boss calls you into the office to scold you for your latest mistake, he is ____ .

   (a) biting off more than he can chew (手に余るような仕事をやろうとする)
   (b) chewing the fat = talking with somebody,
   (c) chewing the rag (くうをこぼす)
   (d) chewing you out =

_(a)_ 3. If you have "juice" at your place of employment, you ____ .

   (a) have power
   (b) are frustrated with your job
   (c) drink on the job
   (d) are in the prime of your life

_(c)_ 4. Who would be most likely to "ham it up"?

   (a) a freeloader   (c) a showoff
   (b) a scatterbrain   (d) a wallflower

_(d)_ 5. Which score indicates that the Detroit Lions "made mincemeat" out of the Los Angeles Rams?

   (a) 7–0   (b) 7–6   (c) 42–34   (d) 49–6

_(b)_ 6. Which term describes a public eating place where the food is cheap?

   (a) sloppy Joe's   (c) restaurant
   (b) hash house   (d) gyp joint

_(a)_ 7. "Don't you ever have anything besides 'rabbit food' for lunch?" Marsha complained to her husband. Marsha's husband was in the habit of eating ____ for lunch.

   (a) salad   (c) wood shavings
   (b) rabbit stew   (d) grass

_(c)_ 8. "Sorry I'm late, but it's like 'pea soup' out there," explained Mr. Weaver. Mr. Weaver was referring to ____ .

   (a) a hailstorm   (c) a thick fog
   (b) a traffic jam   (d) slippery road conditions

_(a)_ 9. Which phrase means the same thing as the expression "in a jam"?

   (a) "in a pickle"   (c) "in the gravy"   You can't do what you can't do.
   (b) "in a pig's eye"   (d) "out to lunch"

_(b)_   10. Which expression would be good advice for a person who tends to spend much time regretting past mistakes?

      (a) "Butter wouldn't melt in your mouth."
      (b) "Don't cry over spilled milk."
      (c) "If life hands you a lemon, make lemonade."
      (d) "You can't have your cake and eat it too."

_(d)_   11. If you continuously flatter your boss, your fellow workers probably call you _____ .

      (a) a cold fish   (c) a good egg
      (b) a cream puff   (d) an apple polisher

_(c)_   12. When Aunt Betty asked her brother how she was supposed to recognize her nephew whom she'd never met, her brother replied, "Just look for the 'carrot-top'." Aunt Betty's nephew _____ .

      (a) had freckles   (c) was a redhead
      (b) looked like a farmer   (d) wore a green cap

_(c)_   13. Anthony had a "pie-in-the-sky" idea about how to make a lot of money fast. His idea was _____ .

      (a) likely to be successful   (c) not very practical
      (b) to buy a bakery   (d) to put restaurants in airplanes

_(a)_   14. If you decided to go to a diner for breakfast, and you ordered "cackleberries and grunts," the waitress would bring you _____ .

      (a) eggs and bacon
      (b) home fries and corned beef hash
      (c) jelly doughnuts and coffee
      (d) pancakes and sausages

_(a)_   15. The "breadwinner" in the family is the one who _____ .

      (a) "brings home the bacon"
      (b) "lives high off the hog"
      (c) "spills the beans"
      (d) "takes the cake"

Language experts have offered explanations for how many of these terms and expressions have entered our everyday speech. For example, one explanation is offered for an expression which appears in Question 15: At many county fairs, the winner of the greased pig event is allowed to bring home the pig as his prize. _(a)_ Which of the four answer choices in Question 15 best matches this explanation?

4 **More Work with the Plural Possessive.** Because not all plural words in our language end in *s*, it is necessary to learn one more rule for forming plural possessives.

> When the plural word does *not* end in *s*, and you want to indicate ownership, add an *'s* to the word just as you do to form the singular possessive. *Women's* and *oxen's* are two examples of this rule.

Use this rule and the other two rules you have studied to form the possessive forms of the words below. Study the examples in order to help you complete this exercise correctly.

Singular	Singular Possessive	Plural	Plural Possessive
1. cereal	cereal's	cereals	cereals'
2. frontiersman	frontiersman's	frontiersmen	frontiersmen's
3. thief	thief's	thieves	thieves'
4. foreigner	foreigner's	foreigners	foreigners'
5. utensil	utensil's	utensils	utensils'
6. child	child's	children	children's
7. McCormick	McCormick's	McCormicks	McCormicks'
8. Congresswoman	Congresswoman's	Congresswomen	Congresswomen's
9. polisher	polisher's	polishers	polishers'
10. watermelon	watermelon's	watermelons	watermelons'
11. handyman	handyman's	handymen	handymen's
12. district	district's	districts	districts'
13. reservation	reservation's	reservations	reservations'
14. axman	axman's	axmen	axmen's
15. deer	deer's	deer	deer's

5 **The Suffixes** *-ance* **and** *-ence*. One of the most troublesome spelling decisions for many of us is whether to end certain words with *-ance* or *-ence*. Choose the word which best completes each sentence and write it in the blank. Watch your spelling!

1. In "A Breakfast Scene" the _____(c)_____ of Walter's son indicates that the bathroom is now free.

   (a) attendance   (b) disobedience   (c) entrance   (d) obedience

2. In "A Breakfast Scene" Travis's _____(b) (a)_____ is evident when his mother refuses to give him money which the teacher has asked the children to bring in.

   (a) annoyance   (b) disobedience   (c) importance   (d) independence

3. Because of a certain _____(a) (d) = cholestrol_____ in eggs, many physicians encourage their patients to cut down on the number they eat each week, while other physicians contend that eggs are one of our most perfect foods.

   (a) annoyance   (b) appearance   (c) disturbance   (d) substance

4. Diet experts find it tragic that many Americans prefer _____(a)_____ foods which can be prepared and eaten in a hurry rather than healthful foods which often require more time to prepare and consume.

   (a) convenience   (b) excellence   (c) preference   (d) reference

5. The food industry often counts on public _____(c) (b)_____ of good diet practices in order to sell their products.

   (a) admittance   (b) dependence   (c) ignorance   (d) insistence

6. For example, recognizing the _____(b)_____ of breakfast but not giving themselves enough time to eat it, many busy Americans gulp down an instant breakfast drink before dashing off to work or school.

   (a) dependence   (b) importance   (c) excellence   (d) innocence

7. In gulping down these sweet and tasty breakfast treats, consumers are disobeying the health practice of many diet experts: _____(a)_____ of sugar.

   (a) avoidance   (b) convenience   (c) influence   (d) occurrence

8. By almost everyone's standards, a poor diet lowers our _____(d)_____ to colds and other illnesses that may be going around.

   (a) entrance   (b) independence   (c) innocence   (d) resistance

9. Some consumers have lost _____(b)_____ in the food industry not only because of how food is sold, but also because of the way it is grown.

   (a) endurance   (b) confidence   (c) independence   (d) obedience

10. The farmers' attitude may be one of "good _____(c)_____" as they spray their fields with insecticides to protect their crops from pests, but this is not necessarily an intelligent attitude.

    (a) annoyance   (b) resistance   (c) riddance   (d) substance

Lesson 19

Taste Treats

Words for Study

Granola	Inc.	nutritious	emerald
nutrition	harvest	vitamin	nutrients
cultural	mangle	campaign	community
tradition	scientists	preservative	original
imaginary	flavor	label	artificial

Taste Treats

What did you eat for breakfast this morning? A bowl of cereal? A glass of instant breakfast drink? Granola, figs, and goat's milk? What difference does it make anyway? If you're like most people, you just don't think about it.

Few of us have any clear idea of what we really eat, let alone what we need. But most of us *think* we know what's good for us. We consider ourselves experts about our own food, so we latch on to each nutrition fad that hits the headlines, and we gobble up each new taste treat.

On the whole, American "taste treats" consist of soft, rather tasteless foods that all seem to have the same appearance. Sounds pretty boring doesn't it? But we wouldn't continue to eat this way if we didn't like it. How did we learn to like it?

Family style, cultural background, and religious tradition all have some influence on our personal tastes, but to a much larger degree our taste has been shaped by the food business.

The food industry is not in business to insure our proper nutrition. The food industry is in business to sell food. In the marketplace, food is a product, just as sewing machines, shoes, and tractors are products. And like the makers of those other products, the food people have found ways to turn out the maximum number of products for the greatest possible profit.

Beans by the Billion

Let's see how an imaginary food industry manages to guide its business toward greater profit while influencing public food habits and decreasing the nutritional value of the consumer's diet.

Crunchy Bean Inc., CBI for short, wants to sell as many cans of beans as possible. That means it needs a lot of beans to can all year round. CBI either owns or has contracts with hundreds of bean farms in different parts of the country. The cheapest and quickest way to harvest all those beans is by machine, so Crunchy has a special machine built. These machines work fine, but they mangle the beans. So CBI scientists create a seed that produces a bean which is tough enough to be harvested by machine. The new bean doesn't taste quite as good, but it looks better in the can.

There is a certain point at which beans should be picked if they are to provide maximum flavor and nutrition. But CBI must transport its beans long distances, and by the time ripe, nutritious beans reach the cannery, they're beginning to rot. So the company sees to it that the beans are harvested before they are at their peak. That way, the beans will be firm at the cannery but not so rich in vitamin A.

What does this type of operation mean for the consumer's taste and nutrition? It means that if you ate Crunchy green beans, you would be eating food designed for machines, not people. The beans may not taste as good as those grown on a local farm, but the consumer accepts them, because they are more readily available than fresh beans. They aren't bad for you, but they could be better and they could taste better.

Creating a Need

Now, what happens if people don't want to buy all those cans of beans? CBI loses money. The company has to *make* people want to buy its green beans. If most consumers like green beans soft, not crunchy, CBI will begin an advertising campaign designed to convince the public that crunchy canned beans are better than "flabby" ones. If the ads work, the public has been "educated" to believe, rightly or wrongly, that canned beans should be crunchy. Our tastes have changed again.

New and Improved!

If sales pick up, production must be increased. Beans that once could go straight from the trucks into the cans must be kept "fresh" while they wait their turn for processing at the cannery. To keep them green and firm, CBI sprinkles a preservative over its beans. The preservative isn't harmful, but it adds a taste to the beans. And it's not foolproof: while they're sitting, the beans lose a bit more of their nutritional value. Taste changes again, and food value decreases.

Meanwhile, some consumers notice that the beans in the can don't look like the beans on the printed label. The beans in the picture are bright green; the ones in the can aren't. People are complaining. So CBI adds a green dye to its beans to make them match the label. The customers stop complaining. They have learned that canned beans are supposed to be an emerald green. Any company that tries to sell them beans with the slightly gray tone that naturally results from the canning process is out of luck.

What Happened?

Nature started off with a green bean, a good source of vitamin A and other nutrients. Farmers learned to grow that bean, to produce enough to feed a large community during the normal growing season. The beans were flavorful and rich in nutrition. Canning made it possible for a larger group of people to eat green beans all year round. The beans tasted all right and kept much of their original food value.

Then the desire for more and more profit and machines stepped in. In the end, the green-bean public learned to demand canned beans that had been grown tough, picked before they were ripe, and preserved and dyed by artificial means.

What happened to our imaginary bean consumer is what happens to all of us when we buy, taste, eat, and learn to like many of the food products on the market today. Most of the food has been grown for appearance and processed for convenience. Taste and nutrition have been left behind.

Of course, the food-processing system is not all bad. Were it not for mass production and the means of preserving food, we would not have available the wide variety of foods we have today.

But how much *real* variety is there, anyway? Because of the many packages that crowd our supermarket shelves, we tend to think that we have a great deal of choice in what we eat. But is it really true?

We may have seven different flavors of corn chips and more than a hundred different brands of breakfast cereals, but that kind of "choice" does not represent true variety. If you want to buy five unwaxed apples, you will probably have a hard time—usually you must settle for six waxed ones in a plastic package. If you decide to avoid dyes and sugar, you will have to give up much of your standard diet. If you want to buy whole-wheat flour or whole-grain cereals, you have to be prepared to pay a higher price.

The food industry has managed to create thousands of new products and in the process has influenced our tastes and health. As the number of different food products increases, food quality is decreasing and our actual choice of what to eat is becoming more and more limited.

1 **About the Reading.** Put the letter of the correct answer on the line to the left.

_(a)_   1. Generally speaking, the major influence on today's American diet is ____ .

     (a) the food industry   (c) religious tradition
     (b) family style   (d) cultural background

_(d)_   2. Generally speaking, the author finds canned foods to be ____ .

     (a) expensive   (c) nutritious
     (b) foolproof   (d) somewhat tasteless

_(c)_   3. Scientists at the imaginary Crunchy Bean Inc. created their beans for ____ .

     (a) canned goods rich in nutrients
     (b) the consumers' preference for emerald-colored beans
     (c) the machines that harvested them
     (d) the soil in which the beans grew

_(b)_   4. If dye were not added to canned green beans, their color would be slightly ____ .

     (a) black   (c) brown
     (b) gray   (d) blue

_(b)_   5. A major reason that canned beans are popular with the American consumers is that they are ____ .

     (a) a rich source of vitamin A
     (b) available year round
     (c) better in taste and color than fresh green beans
     (d) less expensive than fresh green beans

_(a)_   6. The author uses the example of corn chips as part of her argument to show that ____ .

     (a) there is not so much variety in the American diet as we think
     (b) Americans prefer snack foods which are high in nutrients
     (c) the food industry competes heavily for shelf space in the supermarket
     (d) Americans prefer snack foods to nutritious foods

_(d)_   7. If the consumer wants to buy food that is considered to be higher in nutritional value, he will ____ .

     (a) be out of luck
     (b) completely avoid canned goods
     (c) have little difficulty finding the item he desires
     (d) probably have to pay more

_(b)_
_(a)_   8. In the section entitled "Creating a Need," the author wrote "...the public has been 'educated'..." The reason she put _educated_ in quotes is that she is ____ .

     (a) drawing readers' attention to this word so they will remember the point she is making
     (b) pointing out that _educating_ the public often means _fooling_ them
     (c) quoting from another author's book about nutrition
     (d) using an important advertising term to show that she knows what she is talking about

<u>(c)</u>   9. The author of this reading passage seems to believe that most of us ____ .

(a) are too intelligent to be influenced by the food industry
(b) don't care whether or not we are eating nutritious food
(c) have little idea of the extent to which our taste is influenced by the food industry
(d) know what kinds of food we should eat

2 What Do You Think? Answer the following questions in good sentence form. Be sure to offer support for your answers.

1. The reading passage comes from a book titled *You Are What You Eat*, which was published in 1977. Do you think the facts and ideas presented in this book or other books that deal with the subject of diet have had any effect on either the food industry or consumers?

   I think they have had a little effect. For example there are organic corners in some grocery stores, and it means that some people care about good health.

2. Based on what you've read, do you think you will try to become a better informed food consumer?

   Yes. I knew that most apples were waxed, but didn't know that canned beans were dyed. I need more information about food industry.

3 **A Taste Test**. There are four basic tastes: sweet, salty, bitter, and sour. Classify the food items listed below according to these tastes.

bacon	cream puffs	lemon peel	sauerkraut
baking chocolate	doughnuts	lime juice	smoked ham
coffee cake	grapefruit	mustard greens	soy sauce
corned beef	hot chocolate	orange rind 皮	vinegar

Sweet

1. _coffee cake_
2. _cream puffs_
3. _doughnuts_
4. _hot chocolate_

Salty

1. _bacon_
2. _corned beef_
3. _smoked ham_
4. _soy sauce_

Bitter

1. _baking chocolate_
2. _lemon peel_
3. _orange rind_
4. _mustard greens_

Sour

1. _grapefruit_
2. _lime juice_
3. _sauerkraut_
4. _vinegar_

Which of these four tastes is your favorite? _____Sweet._____

Do you think the food industry has influenced you in preferring this taste? Explain.

Yes. When it sells cake, it adds much sugar, and sugar is added in juice, too.

4 **Word Families.** Use the words listed at the left to complete these sentences correctly.

nutrition 知所
nutritious
nutrients

1. Mrs. Chapman thought she was feeding her family _nutritious_ meals until she read a book about _nutrients_ (*nutrition*) and realized that her recipes were lacking in many important _nutrition_ (*nutrients*).

entertain
entertainment
entertainer

2. The _entertainer_ was tired of spending every weekend providing _entertainment_ for others, and he wished someone would come along who would _entertain_ him for a change.

convenience
convenient
conveniently

3. JoAnne loved _convenient_ (*convenience*) foods such as TV dinners so much that she _conveniently_ forgot her doctor's warning that her stomach did not find a steady diet of this food _convenience_ (*convenient*) to manage.

practical
practically
impractical

4. Mr. Lash was _practically_ finished with the blueprints for the new shopping mall when he realized that they were so _impractical_ that he'd have to start all over again and come up with a more _practical_ design.

possessed
possession
possessive

5. Anthony was not normally a _possessive_ person, but he valued his cabin cruiser so much that he would let his friends borrow anything else he _possessed_ just as long as they didn't so much as touch his beloved _possession_.

confided
confidence
confidential

6. Bart was sure that he was doing the right thing as he told the police officer in a _confidential_ tone of voice the location of the stolen loot which his brother had _confided_ to him in total _confidence_.

created
creator
creation
creative

7. Standing before the painting in the lobby, the hotel guest exclaimed, "Who _created_ this mess!" whereupon the _creator_, who just happened to be standing nearby, said sharply, "Madam, the fact that you cannot see this is a wonderful _creation_ shows that you totally lack a _creative_ mind!"

obey
obedience
obedient
obediently

8. Mrs. Wicker couldn't understand how her boxer could ___*obey*___ every single command at ___*obedience*___ school when, at home, he was not at all ___*obedient*___ , in spite of the fact that she ___*obediently*___ followed the trainer's instructions.

science
scientist
scientific
scientifically

9. "You may be a great ___*scientist*___ who has done much to advance the goals of ___*science*___ in our time," snapped Mr. Beaumont at his wife. "But when it comes to ___*scientifically*___ managing the family budget, you're about as ___*scientific*___ as a fortune cookie!"

indifferent
indifferently
indifference

10. Filled with ___*indifference*___ about what to eat for supper after a hectic day at work, Donald ___*indifferently*___ cracked two eggs into a bowl and was completely ___*indifferent*___ to the shocked look on his wife's face as he ate them raw.

5 **Review of the Apostrophe.** In each sentence, only one of the underlined words needs an apostrophe. Circle that word and then write it correctly on the line to the left. Sometimes you need to write the singular possessive, and sometimes you need to write the plural possessive. Study the example before you begin.

cents'   1. With only fifty <u>cents</u> in his pocket, Junior bought fifty (cents) worth of bubble gum at the candy store.

sausages'   2. As Mrs. Sears prepared the <u>sausages</u> for dinner, she hoped that the <u>sausages</u> taste would be as wonderful as their smell.

Scientists'   3. <u>Scientists</u> discoveries are sometimes later regretted by the <u>scientists</u> themselves when they see how people abuse their findings for profit rather than use them for the common good.

days'   4. "What do you expect?" said the supervisor to the angry worker. "You work for two <u>days</u>, and you get two <u>days</u> pay."

trucker's   5. When the <u>truckers</u> favorite diner was suddenly invaded by a busload of Girl Scouts, he was sure they were unaware that this particular eating place catered to <u>truckers</u>.

warrior's   6. The <u>warriors</u> confidence was so great that he was able to defeat the enemy <u>warriors</u> despite being outnumbered.

Joneses'   7. There were so many <u>Joneses</u> listed in the telephone book that Willy didn't know which of the <u>Joneses</u> numbers to try first.

boy's   8. Hearing her youngest <u>boys</u> laughter in the next room, Rosella shrugged her shoulders and sighed, "<u>Boys</u> will be <u>boys</u>!"

noodles'   9. Having decided the <u>noodles</u> shape was all wrong for the tuna fish dish she was preparing, Joan returned to the grocery store and bought a package of flat egg <u>noodles</u>.

emeralds'   10. The jewelry thief was outraged when he found out that the <u>emeralds</u> he had stolen were artificial and only the <u>emeralds</u> settings were worth any money.

6 **Can You Crack the Code?** Each group of letters on the left spells the name of a jewel, but the name has been concealed by a code in which different letters have been used. The code is the same for all the jewels. When you have guessed a jewel, fill in the letters and use these letters for the other jewels until you have cracked the code for the entire group. Use the facts about the jewels to help you crack the code.

1. Y D Y G S I U
   EMELALD

The May birthstone, this gem is a symbol of success. Crunchy Inc. made its green beans look like this beautiful jewel on the label of its cans.

2. G J C O
   RUBY

If Crunchy Inc. started selling beets, they might use the color of this gem for the label. A symbol of safety, the Greeks believed "July children" wearing this jewel could go anywhere and not be harmed.

3. N Y S G I
   PEARL

Formed inside the shells of oysters, this gem is soft and can be easily scratched. One of the June birthstones, this jewel is a symbol of health.

4. U V S D B W U
   DIAMOND

Thousands of years ago, the people in Egypt began the tradition of setting these sparkling jewels in wedding rings. A symbol of love that stays young forever, this gem is the April birthstone.

5. L B N S A
   TOPAZ

The value of this gemstone depends on its quality, not its size. It is a symbol of faithfulness and the November birthstone.

6. B N S I
   OPAL

A symbol of hope, this gem is a milky white with a rainbow of colors. It is one of the October birthstones.

7. F S N N Q V G Y
   SAPPHIRE

Second only to the diamond in hardness, this gem is used as a needle in phonographs. This September birthstone is a symbol of mental and moral well-being.

8. C I B B U F L B W Y
   BLOODSTONE

This gem is one of the birthstones for people born in the month of March. It is a symbol of courage.

9. S D Y L Q O F L
   AMETHYST

The purple color of this gem is believed to be caused by impure substances such as iron. A symbol of being truthful, this jewel is the February birthstone.

10. K S G W Y L
    GARNET

This gem ranges in color from red, brown and black to different shades of yellow and green. It is a symbol of loyalty and the January birthstone.

11. L J G H J B V F Y
    TURQUOISE

Many artificial versions of this stone are produced. This bright blue to blue-green stone is the December birthstone and a symbol of wealth.

12. F S G U B W O P
    SARDONYX

Used in rings and other jewelry, this jewel is one of the cheaper gem stones. One of the August birthstones, it is a symbol of happiness.

Lesson 20

The Wizard of Alabama

Words for Study

wizard	Tuskegee	dairy	concocted
stunningly	laboratory	testify	patents
cosmetics	fulfill	Senate	secrets
axle	compatibility	committee	dynamite
Missouri	agricultural	snubbed	odorless
transferred	whereas	presentation	element

The Wizard of Alabama

Born sometime during the Civil War, George Washington Carver overcame the handicap of his slave background to be praised in his own lifetime as an outstanding scientist. During a stunningly creative career, Carver turned the lowly peanut, considered useful only as hog food, and the unknown sweet potato into hundreds of separate products, ranging from cosmetics and axle grease to printer's ink and coffee.

From the time he was able to get about by himself in the countryside, young Carver began to display a remarkable knowledge of all growing things. Local farmers in Diamond Grove, a tiny community in southwestern Missouri, remembered the weak-looking boy wandering about for hours, examining plants, and bringing back certain varieties with which he could heal sick animals. Farmers' wives from all over the countryside brought him their ailing house plants, begging him to make them bloom. When he returned the plants to their owners and was asked repeatedly how he could work his miracles, Carver only said softly: "All flowers talk to me and so do hundreds of little living things in the woods. I learn what I know by watching and loving everything."

Enrolling in a small college in Iowa, Carver supported himself by doing laundry for students. Later he transferred to the Iowa State College of Agriculture. There his best-loved teacher taught him that nations last only as long as their topsoil. Carrying a heavy load of course work, Carver, a self-taught organist, paid for his education by playing the organ in local churches.

By 1896, Carver had his master's degree and was invited to teach at the college. However, when Booker T. Washington asked him to come to Tuskegee, Alabama, and head his school's department of agriculture, Carver decided to accept. He turned down the well-paying post in Iowa for the opportunity to serve his own people.

Carver had not been in Tuskegee more than a few weeks when he realized that the main problem facing the flat land spreading out in hundreds of square miles around him was its slow poisoning through planting year in year out a single crop—cotton—which for generations had been sucking the life out of the soil. He set up a private laboratory, christened "God's Little Workshop," in which he would sit for hours with plants and into which he never allowed a single book to enter.

For his students at Tuskegee he made his lectures as simple yet as thorough as possible. They were greatly impressed that Carver would rise at four o'clock each morning to walk in the woods before the start of the working day and bring back countless plants for his lectures.

Adaptation of "The Wizard of Tuskegee" from *The Secret Life of Plants* by Peter Tompkins & Christopher Bird. Copyright © 1973 by Peter Tompkins. Reprinted by permission of Harper & Row, Publishers, Inc.

Explaining this habit to friends, Carver said, "Nature is the greatest teacher and I learn from her best when others are asleep. In the still dark hours before sunrise God tells me of the plans I am to fulfill."

The plan Carver fulfilled for which he is perhaps best remembered was his work with the peanut. Late one evening while studying the peanut in his workshop, Carver stared at a peanut plant and asked, "Why did the Lord make you?" In a flash, he received the shortest of answers. "You have three things to go by: compatibility, temperature, and pressure."

With this slim advice, Carver locked himself in his laboratory. There, throughout a sleepless week, he began breaking down the peanut into its parts and exposing them to different conditions of temperature and pressure. Working round the clock, he finally had two dozen bottles, each containing a brand-new product.

Leaving his laboratory, he called a meeting of farmers and agricultural experts and showed them what he had done. He begged his audience to plow under the soil-destroying cotton and plant peanuts instead, telling them that it would produce a cash crop of far more value than its sole existing use as food for pigs might indicate.

The audience was doubtful. To set their minds at ease, Carver began to issue bulletins. In one bulletin, he stated that a rich and healthful butter could be made from the peanut, and that whereas it took one hundred pounds of dairy milk to make ten pounds of butter, a hundred pounds of peanuts could produce thirty-five pounds of peanut butter. Other bulletins showed how many, many products could be extracted from the sweet potato, a vine which most Americans had never heard of.

By 1930, the peanut's one-time worthlessness had been turned into a huge, successful industry, and peanut butter became one of the favorite foods of even the poorest American child. In the middle of the Great Depression, Carver was called to Washington to testify before a Senate committee. Dressed in his usual two-dollar black suit, with an ever-present flower in its buttonhole and a homemade necktie, Carver, upon arriving at Union Station, was snubbed by a waiting porter who, when Carver asked him to help with his bags and direct him to Congress, replied, "Sorry, Pop, I ain't got time for you now. I'm expecting an important colored scientist coming from Alabama." Patiently, Carver carried his own bags to a taxi which took him to Capitol Hill.

The Senate committee had allowed him no more than ten minutes to testify. But when he began his presentation and took from his bag the countless creations concocted in his laboratory, the vice president of the United States overruled the timetable and told Carver he could have as much time as he liked because his presentation was the best that he had ever seen given to a Senate committee.

In half a lifetime of research Carver, though he created fortunes for thousands, rarely made much money from any of his ideas. When people reminded him of the money he might have made had he only protected himself with patents, he replied simply, "God did not charge me or you for making peanuts. Why should I profit from their products?" Thomas Edison told people that "Carver is worth a fortune" and backed up his statement by offering to employ the black scientist at an extremely high salary. Carver turned down the offer. Henry Ford, who thought Carver "the greatest scientist living," tried to get him to work for him with an equal lack of success.

Because people did not understand the source from which his magic with plant products sprang, they did not understand his methods either. Visitors to his laboratory would find Carver puttering at his workbench cluttered with molds, soils, plants, and insects. The visitors were puzzled by his simple replies to their persistent pleas for him to reveal his secrets. To one puzzled interviewer, he said: "The secrets are in the plants. To learn them, you have to love them enough."

"But why do so few people have your power?" the man persisted. "Who besides you can do these things?"

"Everyone can," said Carver, "if only they believe it." Tapping a large Bible on a table he added, "The secrets are all here. In God's promises. These promises are real, as real as and more solid than this table."

1 **About the Reading.** Use information from the reading to complete these statements.

1. George Washington Carver was considered "the wizard from Alabama" because _he could heal sick animals with plants, and make ailing plants bloom._

2. Before Carver's time, Americans did not eat peanuts because _they were considered useful only as hog food._

3. Before Carver's time, Americans did not eat sweet potatoes because _it was unknown._

4. Carver turned down an offer to teach at Iowa State College because _he realized that the main problem facing Tuskegee was cotton, which was poisoning the soil._

5. The porter at the train station in Washington, D.C., snubbed Carver because _Carver wasn't well dressed, and the porter didn't know that was Carver._

6. Carver was not interested in making a fortune from his inventions because _he thought that God did not charge him for making peanuts and didn't want to profit from the products._

7. Cite three examples which indicate that Carver had no particular interest in money.
   a. _He turned down the well-paying post in Iowa._
   b. _Thomas Edison backed up an extremely high salary job, but Carver turned down the offer._
   c. _He created fortunes for thousands, rarely made much money from any of his ideas._

8. Carver probably called his laboratory "God's Little Workshop" because _he believed God, and he thought God made him study plants._

9. People were often puzzled by Carver's working methods in his laboratory because _they just found Carver puttering at his workbench cluttered with molds, soils, plants, and insects in his laboratory._

10. Carver believed that anyone could work with plant life the way he himself did if _only they believe the Bible._

2 More Facts about the Peanut. Use the words listed below to complete these facts about the peanut correctly.

groundnuts per cent pods soil

harvested period ripen temperature

machines plants ripened unusual

pegs plows snap usually

More Facts about the Peanut

The peanut is a fruit of the peanut plant. The peanut is a kind of pea, not a nut. Like other peas, peanuts bear seeds in containers called __pods__. There are __usually__ two peanuts in each peanut shell. The peanut plant is __groundnuts__ because its pods grow underground. For this reason, peanuts are often called __pegs__.

Peanut __plants__ grow best in light, well-drained, sandy soil. They need much sunshine, warm __temperature__, and a frost-free growing __period__ of four to five months. Farmers must harvest peanuts at the right time. If they harvest their crops too early, many pods will not have __pegs__. If they harvest them too late, the pegs may __snap__, and many pods will be left in the soil. __Unusual__ are the stalk-like stems of the pods.

Most pods __ripen__ 120 to 150 days after planting. At harvest time, farmers use digging __plows__ to lift the plants from the __soil__. After they have dried, __machines__ called combines remove the pods from the plants.

Throughout the world, from 19 to 22 million short tons of peanuts are __harvested__ each year. Farmers in Asia and Africa grow about 85 __per cent__ of the world's peanuts.

Adapted from *The World Book Encyclopedia.* © 1987 World Book, Inc.

3 Word Relationships.

Word Relationships. On the line at the left, write the letter of the answer that best completes the sentence.

___(b)___ 1. Mumps are to illness as _____ .

    (a) freckles are to nose   (c) orchard is to grove

    (b) lipstick is to cosmetics   (d) peanut is to by-product

___(a)___ (2.) Artificial is to unnatural as _____ .

    (a) consciousness is to awareness   (c) location is to surrounding

    (b) lecture is to speaker   (d) wealth is to well-being

___(b)___ 3. Year is to century as _____ .

    (a) acre is to farm land   (c) meter is to centimeter

    (b) cent is to dollar   (d) September is to autumn

___(c)___ 4. Dissolve is to harden as _____ .

    (a) adapt is to conform   (c) approach is to snub

    (b) ripen is to harvest   (d) transform is to transfer

___(d)___ 5. Congressman is to Capitol Hill as _____ .

    (a) organist is to organ   (c) striker is to picket line

    (b) weaver is to blanket   (d) scientist is to laboratory

___(b)___ 6. Medium is to average as _____ .

    (a) adventuresome is to restless   (c) costly is to impractical

    (b) convenient is to handy   (d) respected is to beloved

___(c)___ 7. Grape is to raisin as _____ .

    (a) juice is to snack   (c) plum is to prune

    (b) vine is to garden   (d) lemon is to lemonade

___(d)___ 8. Pear is to pare as _____ .

    (a) eating is to baking   (c) fruit is to peeler

    (b) farmer is to cook   (d) knead is to need

homonymn

___(a)___ 9. Natural is to manmade as _____ .

    (a) wilderness is to settlement   (c) pigtail is to wig

    (b) groundnut is to peanut   (d) steer is to dairy cow

___(d)___ 10. Plant is to uproot as _____ .

    (a) combine is to tractor   (c) fulfill is to transform

    (b) create is to advertise   (d) restrain is to unleash

4 **The Suffix -ize.** Use the words at the left to complete the sentences correctly.

alphabetized
authorized (授权之)
criticize (批判する)
memorize
modernize
organized (整理する)
recognize
scandalized
specialize
symbolizes
terrorized
tenderized

1. Joan decided to _specialize_ in the care of babies and young children at medical school after she had a lengthy discussion with her advisor.

2. Mr. Crane finally realized that if he didn't _modernize_ the outdated machinery in his factory, he would probably have to shut down the plant before the end of the year.

3. Even though Kitty had _tenderized_ the beef according to the directions, the roast still tasted like shoe leather.

4. Santa Claus, rather than the birth of Jesus, _symbolizes_ the meaning of Christmas for some people in our culture.

5. "I expect you to _memorize_ all fifty state capitals by Wednesday," announced Mr. Chapman to his disbelieving geography class.

6. Even Skip's mother-in-law didn't _recognize_ him after his hair transplant that made him look twenty years younger.

7. "Tomorrow I've got to get _organized_," Johnny muttered to himself upon surveying the pile of dirty laundry in the equally dirty bathroom.

8. "The family will be _scandalized_!" said Betsy upon hearing that Uncle Jay had been arrested for driving in circles on the railroad tracks at two o'clock in the morning.

9. The townspeople were _terrorized_ by widespread reports that a mob of gangsters was planning to set up their headquarters at the local hotel.

10. When the salesclerk said that he wasn't _authorized_ to accept personal checks, the angry customer demanded to see the manager at once.

11. Helen was thankful for the _alphabetized_ list of recipes in the back of her cookbook whenever she wanted to try out a new casserole.

12. "Praise a child seven times a day; _criticize_ only once" was a piece of advice Mrs. Peck tried to follow whenever she was tempted to speak to her children harshly.

5 **Find This Peanut Product.** As you learned in the reading, peanuts are used for many products besides peanut butter. Believe it or not, peanuts can not only fill you up, they can blow you up. To find out how, follow these directions for solving the puzzle.

- Fill in the answers to the definitions by using all the syllables in the box. Use each syllable only once.
- The number after each definition tells you how many syllables are in the word.
- The number of letters in each answer is indicated by the number of blank spaces. Study the example before you begin.
- When the words are correctly filled in, their first letters, reading down, will reveal the name of a peanut product which is used to make one of the substances in dynamite.

a	blad	bon	car	cord	der	di	ex	fec	fu	gall	gen
gurt	hale	hale	ide	in	in	lax	na	nos	ox	ox	rai
rip	sin	sion	tion	tive	trans	tril	vel	y	yo		

n o s t r i l   1. either of the two outer openings of the nose (2)

i n h a l e   2. to breathe in (2)

t r a n s f u s i o n   3. the direct injection of whole blood or another solution into the bloodstream (3)

r i p c o r d   4. a cord pulled to release the pack of a parachute (2)

o x y g e n   5. a colorless, odorless, tasteless element necessary for breathing (3)

g a l l b l a d d e r   6. where bile is stored in your body (3)

l a x a t i v e   7. a drug often taken by people who suffer from constipation (3)

y o g u r t   8. a healthful food prepared from milk curdled by bacteria (2)

c a r b o n   d i o x i d e   9. a colorless, odorless gas formed during breathing (5)

e x h a l e   10. to breathe out (2)

r a i s i n   11. a dried, sweet grape (2)

i n f e c t i o n   12. the invasion of a part of the body by germs (3)

n a v e l   13. a synonym for bellybutton (2)

What is the name of this explosive peanut product?   n i t r o g l y c e r i n

6   **To Look at Any Thing.** Read the poem. Then answer the questions which follow in good sentence form.

To Look at Any Thing
by John Moffitt

To look at any thing,
If you would know that thing,
You must look at it long:
To look at this green and say
'I have seen spring in these
Woods,' will not do—You must
Be the thing you see:
You must be the dark snakes of
Stems and ferny plumes of leaves,
You must enter in
To the small silences between
The leaves,
You must take your time
And touch the very peace
They issue from.

1. According to the poet, how do most of us see the world around us?

   We don't see things for a long time.

2. According to the poet, what must we do to really know a thing?

   We must look at a thing long.

3. Cite an example from the reading which indicates that George Washington Carver practiced the advice which the poet offers.

   The secrets are in the plants.

4. Based on the reading, what would George Washington Carver say that we must do in addition to following the poet's advice if we really want to know a thing?

   Believe God.

Review: Lessons 1-20

1 **Word Review.** Use the words listed below to fill in the blanks.

agriculture   frontier   nutrient   profession   transmission
blueprint   inflation   patent   Senate   utensil
compatibility miracle   preservative tradition   wizard

preservative   1. a chemical used in foods to prevent spoilage

patent   2. a grant made by a government to an inventor, securing him the sole right to make, use, and sell his invention for a certain period of time

wizard   3. a skillful or clever person; a magician; a male witch

nutrient   4. a substance in food which is necessary for life and growth

miracle   5. an event that cannot be explained by the laws of nature and so is believed to be supernatural or an act of God

profession   6. an occupation requiring training and advanced study in a specialized field

utensil   7. any instrument or container, especially one used in a kitchen or on a farm

inflation   8. any unusual increase in available money beyond the amount of available goods, resulting in a sharp and continuing rise in price levels

frontier   9. land just beyond or at the edge of a settled area; a border between two countries or the area along it

blueprint   10. plans or drawings which appear as white lines on a blue background; any carefully designed plan

compatibility   11. the ability to live or act peacefully

transmission   12. the gears and related parts of an automobile by which power is sent from the engine to a driving axle; a system of gears

tradition   13. the passing down of elements of a culture from generation to generation

agriculture   14. the science, art and business of planting crops and raising livestock useful to man

Senate   15. the upper house of Congress in the United States to which two members are elected from each state by popular vote for a six-year term

2 Which Word Does Not Fit? Choose the word which does not fit with the rest of the words in each line and write it to the right.

1. pajamas   bathrobe   slippers   nightgown   Windbreaker   _Windbreaker_

2. save   deserve   reserve   conserve   preserve   _deserve_

3. numb (かンかン, 鈍い)   edgy (先のとがった, いらだった)   nervous   tense   upset   _numb_

4. Arctic   Indian   Pacific   Atlantic   Mediterranean   ~~Indian~~ Mediterranean (others are oceans)

5. crisis   crossroad   emergency   starvation (飢え)   zero hour (行動発起時刻)   ~~crossroad~~ zero hour (others are bad things)

6. honor   praise   applause   salary   compliment (賞替)   _salary_

7. Rome   Paris   Moscow   Warsaw   Los Angeles   _Los Angeles_ (others are capitals)

8. loyal (忠義な)   dutiful   faithful   obedient   hardworking   _hardworking_

9. curb (引き留める)   limit   reject   confine (制限する)   restrain   _reject_

10. plague (伝染病)   sorrow   distress (苦悩)   suffering   heartbreak   _plague_

11. clever   valued   creative   skilled   resourceful   _valued_

12. secret   unknown   stunning   mysterious   unexplained   _stunning_

13. apple   peach   turnip (カブ)   grapefruit   raspberry   _turnip_

14. Adams   Jackson   Kennedy   Franklin   Lincoln   _Franklin_

15. gold   opal   topaz   turquoise   amethyst   _gold_

3 **Word Study.** Use the words listed at the left to complete these sentences.

emergency
endure
nagging
plagued
whereupon

1. _Plagued_ by a _nagging_ toothache, Terry could no longer _endure_ the pain, _whereupon_ she phoned the dentist for an _emergency_ appointment.

authorize
classified
creative
opportunities
outraged

2. Hiram was so ~~creative~~ _outraged_ when his boss refused to _authorize_ his latest project that he began to check the ~~outraged~~ _classified_ ads for more ~~classified~~ _creative_ employment _opportunities_.

assistant
assumed
concocted
explanation
scientist

3. The _scientist_ _assumed_ that the solution he'd _concocted_ in his laboratory would still be there the following morning; but it had strangely disappeared, and his _assistant_ could offer no helpful _explanation_ regarding its whereabouts.

advice
advised
device
devise
revise

4. "Take my _advice_ and _devise_ a less costly method for producing this _device_," _advised_ Ms. Franklin's supervisor, "or I'll have to _revise_ the entire budget for your project."

desperate
dutiful
foul
injected
oppression

5. So ~~oppression~~ _desperate_ were the formerly _dutiful_ servants to put an end to the king's ~~foul~~ _oppression_ that they _injected_ poison in the roast being prepared for his supper, hoping that he would not suspect ~~desperate~~ _foul_ play.

confident
detract [dɪtrækt] (働) なくす (けなす)
envy
formally
formerly

6. When he was _____formally_____ appointed stage manager, Alexis—who had _____formerly_____ been "just one of the boys"—was _____confident_____ that any _____envy_____ the other crew members might feel toward him wouldn't _____detract_____ from the many friendships he had at the theater.

accommodate [əkɑ́mədeɪt] (働) ～を収容する
limit
maximum
minimum
resume

7. Because interest in river travel in winter was at a _____minimum_____, the owners of a steamboat which could *accommodate* _____limit_____ a _____maximum_____ of eighty passengers decided to _____resume_____ the number of cruises to two and *limit* _____accommodate_____ their regular number of runs in the spring.

unfruitful
unknown
unlike
unpleasant
unusually

8. The board chairman thought it was _____unlike_____ anything he had ever seen; but for some _____unknown_____ reason, everyone was so _____unpleasant_____ that Thursday afternoon that the meeting was not only _____unusually_____ lengthy but also totally _____unfruitful_____.

4   **Review of Compound Words.** Put the letter of the correct answer on the line to the left.

___(b)___   1.   Which word is related to the activities of Sally Ride?
       (a) handicraft   (b) spacecraft   (c) witchcraft   (d) woodcraft

___(b)___   2.   What would cause a gangster to think he is being tailed?
       (a) doorsteps   (b) footsteps   (c) insteps   (d) sidesteps

___(d)___   3.   Which word is a synonym for *limelight*?
       (a) candlelight   (b) floodlight   (c) gaslight   (d) spotlight

___(a)___   4.   If you lived on a small island and grew tired of seeing the same old faces, where might you go for a change?
       (a) mainland   (b) mainspring   (c) mainstay   (d) mainstream

___(c)___   5.   Which word is a synonym for *positively*?
       (a) downpour   (b) downswing   (c) downright   (d) downturn

___(a)___   6.   Which word refers to a painted curtain hung at the back of a stage set?
       (a) backdrop   (b) backrest   (c) backside   (d) backstage

___(b)___   7.   If you disliked seafood, which of these would you avoid?
       (a) brownstones   (b) cherrystones   (c) gallstones   (d) gemstones

___(a)___   8.   Which word describes a temporary lack of consciousness?
       (a) blackout   (b) blowout   (c) brownout   (d) whiteout

___(a)___   9.   Which of the following is a synonym for *disadvantage* or *inconvenience*?
       (a) drawback   (b) greenback   (c) hunchback   (d) tailback

___(b)___   10.   Which word is a slang synonym for *first-rate*?
       (a) applejack   (b) crackerjack   (c) lumberjack   (d) steeplejack

___(c)___   11.   If your day has run like _____ , everything has gone without a hitch.
       (a) piecework   (b) groundwork   (c) clockwork   (d) teamwork

___(c)___   12.   Since you have only two more exercises to complete in this reading book, you could say that you are in the _____ .
       (a) homecoming   (b) homeroom   (c) homestretch   (d) homework

5 **Review of Contractions.** Write the contractions for the following words on the lines to the right. Study the example before you begin.

1. he is _____ he's _____
2. they will _____ they'll _____
3. does not _____ doesn't _____
4. we have _____ we've _____
5. you had _____ you'd _____
6. I would _____ I'd _____
7. had not _____ hadn't _____
8. will not _____ won't _____
9. she has _____ she's _____
10. you will _____ you'll _____

11. do not _____ don't _____
12. I will _____ I'll _____
13. what is _____ what's _____
14. they had _____ they'd _____
15. there is _____ there's _____
16. she would _____ she'd _____
17. I am _____ I'm _____
18. let us _____ let's _____
19. he had _____ he'd _____
20. madam _____ ma'am _____

6 **Review of Facts and Opinions.** Write *fact* on the line to the left if the statement is a fact. Write *opinion* if the statement is an opinion.

_____*fact*_____ 1. John Quincy Adams was the sixth president of the United States.

_____*fact*_____ 2. Movies have been around longer than peanut butter.

_____*opinion*_____ 3. A brownstone is more beautiful than a tombstone.

_____*fact*_____ 4. South Carolina became a state before Missouri did.

_____*opinion*_____ 5. South Carolina is a more interesting state to visit than Missouri.

_____*fact*_____ 6. There are more motorists on the highway now than there were twenty-five years ago.

_____*fact*_____ 7. The motorists in Boston have a higher accident rate than the motorists in Salt Lake City.

_____*opinion*_____ 8. Some people believe that America's space program is too costly.

_____*fact*_____ 9. More women have been elected to Congress since 1960 than before 1960.

_____*opinion*_____ 10. The life of a congresswoman is more difficult than that of a congressman.

_____*fact*_____ 11. Several lessons in this reading book have offered advice about getting a job.

_____*opinion*_____ 12. Completing the readings and exercises in this reading book has been a lot of fun.